To Liz,
Blessings
David Raynor

One School & Two Families

One School
and
Two Families

David Raynor

Copyright © David Raynor 2025
Produced in association with

The right of David Raynor to be identified as the
Author of this Work has been asserted by him in accordance
with the Copyright, Designs and Patents Act 1988.

All rights reserved. No part of this publication may be
reproduced, stored in a retrieval system, or transmitted, in
any form or by any means, electronic, mechanical,
photocopying, recording or otherwise,
without the prior permission of Words by Design.

ISBN: 978-1-914002-55-7

Typeset in Cambria and Perpetua

Printed and bound in the UK
www.wordsbydesign.co.uk

Cover design by Camron Prince

The White Gates – the entrance to Scarisbrick Hall School

Dedication

To Gwen, Tim and John,
who survived having a headmaster living in their home.

Contents

	Acknowledgements	xi
	A Message from the Headley Family	xii
	Foreword	xiii
	Preface	xv
1	A School in a Mansion	1
2	The Early Years	11
3	Expansion into the Seventies	33
4	Ten Years On	47
5	Into the Eighties	61
6	A Pioneer Passes On	71
7	The Nineties	85
8	The Bombshell	109
9	Renaissance	119
10	High Hopes	135
11	Pandemic Problems	151
12	Looking Ahead	157

Acknowledgements

I am indebted to Rachel Oxley and other members of her family for their help in correcting errors in the first draft of this book.

I am grateful to Charles, Muriel, and Rachel Oxley for their vision, energy and unflagging commitment to building up the school from its inception; also, to Michael and Linda Headley and their family for not only saving the Hall and the school, but developing the whole project to new levels of excellence.

My thanks to Jeff Shaw, former pupil, now Headmaster, for guiding the school through its renewal phase and leading it into an exciting future.

To those former pupils who kindly sent me their recollections of the early years of the school – thank you!

It has been an unexpected delight to renew acquaintance with Susie Gordon Yavetz. (Another former pupil, Susie was my Maria alongside Jeff Shaw's Captain von Trapp in *The Sound of Music* in 1997) Her editorial skills, founded on her excellence in English during her schooldays, have been a great help in the final stages of publication.

Grateful thanks also to Raymond Pelekamoyo, the school's alumni connections administrator, for his help in bringing the book to publication.

*

A Message from the Headley Family

The Headley family would like to express our gratitude to Mr David Raynor for taking the time to document the history of the school over the last sixty years.

As a family we remain steadfast in our commitment to the long-term, evolving, fifty-year vision of what Scarisbrick Hall and School can become. As David describes in this book, the first fifteen years of our journey with Scarisbrick Hall have been focused on restoring the building to its former glory, and, through the continued excellent work of Jeff Shaw and his team, creating an educational model regarded as best in class both in terms of academic results and the development of the whole child through the RIVER learning philosophy, Innovative Wellbeing program and Pastoral Care.

In our anniversary year we are thankful to all those staff, pupils and families who have played a role in Scarisbrick Hall over the last sixty years and hope through our ever-increasing alumni engagement activity we can reconnect with all generations of former pupils and friends of Scarisbrick Hall to strengthen the connection between those who have pride in the shared educational journey they have taken.

We also look to the future and the many milestones we have still to achieve in our vision of Scarisbrick Hall School being recognised internationally for its educational excellence and facilities.

Foreword

It is my privilege to have attended Scarisbrick Hall School as a pupil. In my time at the school I experienced the leadership of the Oxley family and David Raynor, and in my present job I have the honour of working with the present owners, the Headley family.

The school that you attend has a great influence over your life; it is almost as if the DNA of the school somehow seeps into your own, and remains with you throughout the rest of your life. The words that teachers spoke to me remain in a very deep part of my soul, resurfacing when needed. In more practical terms your school is always noted on an application form for a job (no matter how old you are!), so employers and colleagues will therefore naturally make a judgment about the kind of person you are, based on the school that you attended.

At Scarisbrick Hall, we often have alumni visiting the school, asking about the history and journey that it has gone on. It is quite natural for different people to have varying accounts and memories (often recalling some of the mischief they got up to, especially the boarders!). However, there seemed to be a need to pull together a factually accurate account of the school that bridges the two eras of Oxley and Headley.

When one meets one's former Headmaster, there is a kind of magic that transports you back to your childhood. Although we are roughly the same height, he still feels taller and I still sit up straight when he addresses me. Never more so was this true than when I was sat in my study (formerly his) after an update about the school. It was at this time that I posed the question about David writing a book. Knowing that he had written *The Standard Bearer* (a biography of Charles Oxley) - an excellent read for those who have not done so - I had solid evidence that David was the best person to knit the history of the school into not only a coherent, but an engaging piece of work.

To my delight he said yes, and the result is what you are about to read. For me it is an incredibly engaging and insightful story of my school, a school with values engrained in the very fabric of the building, founded on a vision from a remarkable couple and evolved by an inspirational family. The journey from 1964 to the present day makes me proud to be not only the Headmaster but a former pupil of Scarisbrick Hall School.

David has always been an inspiring man both as a teacher and into retirement and I would like to thank him for his time and insight that has brought this into fruition. I hope that you find it as engaging as I did. I recall a moment in a Senior School English lesson taught by David where we were instructed on how to take care of a reading book that we had been issued with. We were told to take great care of the spine and treasure the pages. I certainly will with this one.

Jeff Shaw, Headmaster, Scarisbrick Hall School

Preface

There are those who dream, and there are those who apply everything they have to seeing their dream fulfilled.

The story of Scarisbrick Hall School is largely a tale of two families: the Oxleys and the Headleys. Charles Oxley, at the age of 26, had, with his wife Muriel, already set up a day school, Tower College, in Rainhill in 1948, but also had the vision to establish an evangelical Christian boarding school for boys somewhere in the north of England. It took fifteen years for that dream to become reality. Charles, Muriel and their daughter Rachel each successively served as Principal of both Tower College and Scarisbrick Hall School over a period of thirty-four years. They also embarked on a further venture in 1983, opening a third school in Hamilton, south-east of Glasgow. Financial pressures led the second generation of the Oxley family finally to sell Scarisbrick, which then lost its unique character in an amalgamation. The next twelve years brought changes of ownership and lack of investment that almost resulted in the school's closure.

It was the Headley family who set about restoring both the building and the school to their former glories. Mike Headley and his wife Linda had a granddaughter, Jade, in the Junior School when a merger with Kingswood School in Birkdale virtually brought an end to so much of what Scarisbrick Hall School had represented. The merger, in 1998, appeared to many to be a takeover by a company called Nord Anglia. What happened between then and 2009 is largely outside the remit of this book, but we shall follow the Headley family link through to the new regime. The combined schools had become Kingswood College at Scarisbrick Hall, the change of name reflecting a change of emphasis. Not until the Headley family took over the reins did Scarisbrick Hall School regain its name and begin to re-establish what the Oxley family had built.

CHAPTER 1
A School in a Mansion

Scarisbrick Hall is a 150-room mansion in a rural setting of parkland and woodland, surrounded by wide acres of rich farmland. As far back as 1238 there are records of the Scarisbrick family being given the estate on which the Hall now stands. Although the family's original home is not mentioned, we do know that a substantial house was built at the end of the sixteenth century by Edward Scarisbrick. It was in the nineteenth century that Charles Scarisbrick, followed after his death by his sister, Lady Ann, employed the Pugins as architects and designers to erect and adorn the neo-Gothic edifice that now houses the school.

Although a school did not officially begin to operate at Scarisbrick Hall until 1964, the Hall itself had witnessed educational activity for several centuries. Some might say that God had his eye on the place all along. The Scarisbrick family were staunch Roman Catholics, and from Elizabethan times until 1774 it became a tradition for a priest to live at the Hall, providing services of an educational as well as a spiritual kind for local Catholic families. Some of the Scarisbrick family menfolk themselves went to France to train as Jesuits. That created danger. When the English monarchy was Protestant, questions were asked about Catholic priests. When it was not just the Channel that divided England from France, where did a French-trained priest's loyalties lie? And who could claim the stronger allegiance – the monarch in England or the Pope in Rome?

A secret Roman Catholic school actually operated inside Scarisbrick Hall from the late sixteenth century until the early eighteenth. By that time, the local Church of England vicar and his bishop were willing to turn a blind eye to what was going on. Mona Duggan, in her book *A History of Scarisbrick*, quotes Bishop Porteous of Chester in 1779 writing that 'if ... the schools and mass houses so much complained of, are only frequented by persons of the Roman Catholic persuasion ... and no doctrines are taught hostile to the government of the country, I do not see how on the principles of toleration and of Christianity, any other opposition can be made to them.'

The Education Act of 1870 required sufficient schools to be established in each area to provide elementary education for all children. Churches and the state worked together in the township of Scarisbrick to set up St Mary's, St Mark's, and what is now Pinfold primary schools; and from the Scarisbrick family at the Hall came either the land, or the actual buildings or some funding for these schools. The Hall grounds were also thrown open for the schoolchildren to enjoy special celebrations, such as the end of the First World War.

It was at the end of the Second World War in 1945 that the Scarisbrick family finally left the Hall after 700 years of residence. Death duties were the main reason for their departure. The Church of England bought the premises and the central acreage of the estate in order to establish a teacher training college, St Katherine's. Teaching the teachers continued from 1946 until 1963, when the college moved to premises in Liverpool. But during those years, £250,000 had been spent on the Hall itself and on adding to its facilities. Tennis courts and sports grounds were laid out. In the courtyard area, new buildings provided a chapel, a gymnasium, a dining hall, and boarding accommodation. In addition, the Hall now had the benefit of central heating and modern kitchen equipment.

The reason for the college's move to Liverpool was the recommendation in the 1963 Robbins Report on Higher Education that training colleges with fewer than 200 students were thought to be uneconomical on teaching staff. That definitely applied to St Katherine's, and so the decision was taken to amalgamate the college with another college to form the Liverpool Institute for Higher Education. A further outcome was that Scarisbrick Hall came up for sale.

By the early 1960s, the country had largely shaken off the privations of the post-War years of thrift and rationing. The mood was now being reflected in Harold Macmillan's rather smug declaration to the nation: 'You've never had it so good.' Certainly, there were businessmen with money and ambition who saw the possibilities of a neo-Gothic mansion being turned into a country club with all kinds of leisure facilities. A development company actually bought the estate with the intention of building high-end housing, but the County Planning Authority placed a preservation order on the whole estate because of its outstanding historical and architectural status. The developers had no option but to put the estate up for sale again.

Charles Oxley had served as a fireman in Glasgow and a purser in the Merchant Navy during the Second World War. He then obtained a teaching post at the prestigious Victoria College in Alexandria, Egypt, where his pupils included King Hussein of Jordan, the Sultan of Madagascar, and the son of the Egyptian Prime Minister; but he always had his heart set on a school of his own back in England.

The Education Act of 1944 with selection at 11+ made too arbitrary a distinction, in Charles' eyes, between those children who were expected to cope with an academic education and those who were not. In particular, he believed that the intelligence test was too divisive, consigning those who 'failed' the test to secondary modern schools and those who 'passed' to grammar schools. He was convinced that a good proportion of the boys and girls whose intelligence measurement was below the pass mark would in fact be quite capable of succeeding in a grammar school setting. What these children may have lacked up to the age of 11 was the kind of teaching that would enable them to get through the 11+.

Tower College
What Charles envisaged was a school with high expectations of every child, plus standards of teaching and discipline that would give a sound education and equally sound moral standards, based on the Christian faith. That he was able to start such a school in 1948 says much for his determination and for the patience and diligence of his 22-year-old bride, Muriel. When Charles and Muriel bought The Towers, a substantial mansion in dilapidated condition, Charles still had to serve a term's notice at the school in Egypt, so Muriel was left to deal with builders, plasterers, plumbers, electricians, decorators, and suppliers on her own. The slow speed of letters between Rainhill and Alexandria did not help her at all.

The Oxley brand of education clearly appealed to a wide range of families in the region around St Helens and the eastern fringes of Liverpool. By keeping fees low, Charles and Muriel were able to attract children from families who were prepared to make sacrifices to give their offspring a good education. It was important for the Oxleys to be able to offer places based on a child's merit and potential, rather than the size of the parents' bank balance.

As Tower College grew in numbers and reputation, some parents approached Charles Oxley to ask whether he would consider having boarders. These were mainly Christian missionaries, but also other expatriates who were looking for a boarding school for their children. The premises at Tower College were unsuitable for that purpose, but Charles and Muriel did not dismiss the possibility of starting another school that could accommodate boarders. Local authorities gave grants in those days for the children of expatriates and military personnel to be educated in this country.

By 1963, the Oxleys had fifteen years' experience of running a school, during which time their own three sons and a daughter grew up in The Towers as both school and home. Tower College had been 'recognised as efficient' by the Department for Education, the school had a settled and committed teaching staff, and the results in public examinations were a major attraction for prospective parents.

Curiosity
Whenever small independent schools in the Lancashire and Merseyside area closed down, as quite a number did in the '60s and '70s, Charles and Muriel were always on the lookout for books, furnishings and fittings that could be bought cheaply and put to good use in Tower College. That was one factor in their decision to drive fifteen miles from Rainhill to Scarisbrick one day in 1963. But when they walked round the Hall and saw what the teacher training college had left behind, their eyes – and their dreams – widened considerably.

The property company were keen to sell the Hall and the whole estate, but the Oxleys were only interested in the Hall and its immediate surrounds, so Charles persuaded the vendors to divide up the estate, so that the Hall and the central thirty-eight acres comprised one lot at auction.

Charles and Muriel had a real sense of excitement on the day of the sale. Would their prayers and their hopes win the day? When they arrived, the word was circulating that the Home Office were thinking of the Hall as an approved school for troubled and troublesome boys. Representatives of a well-known holiday camp company were also known to be there for the sale.

Messrs Jackson-Stops of Chester opened the bidding at £10,000, but the price rose above £20,000 before pausing at £24,500. Suddenly, it was all over. The bidding had stopped. The lot was withdrawn, unsold.

Charles' parents had been the proprietors of a large department store in St Helens, so he inherited a certain amount of business acumen in his genes. He knew he had a head start on other potential buyers, because he would not need to apply for change of use to set up an educational establishment. Nevertheless, he was due to fly to India a few days after the unfinished sale of Scarisbrick Hall, so he wasted no time in contacting the property owners and persuading them that he would be willing to take the Hall off their hands for the price at which the bidding had stopped – £24,500 – if they would agree to a quick sale. They did, and he flew off to India with contracts signed, thanking God for what he knew was 'the bargain of the century.'

It was Muriel, however, who had a more sensitive touch on the purse-strings and perhaps a more cautious attitude to the purchase. Her father's photography business, Cholerton's of St Helens, involved all of his six children to one degree or another, and it was Muriel who kept the business thriving through the post-war years, even while Tower College was being established and she was having her family of four children.

Priceless treasures
Included in the September sale of Scarisbrick Hall were carvings, statues, and other art-works that, although they were of great interest and historic value, would have taken the Oxleys' total expenditure well beyond what they could afford. These items were therefore to be sold separately at a later date in November 1963. How they came to remain in situ merits inclusion at this point.

The catalogue for that second sale featured the portrait panels of The King's Room as its first lot, with these words: 'The elder Pugin (Augustus Welby Northmore Pugin, 1812-1852) was one of the great dynamic forces in the history of nineteenth century architecture. He changed the Gothic revival from a fashion to a crusade. Perhaps of all the splendours of Scarisbrick Hall, the King's Room anticipates Pugin's magnificent decoration of the inside of the Houses of Parliament.'

Twenty-seven full-length portraits of Tudor and Stuart kings, queens, and 'notabilities of the court, sumptuously arrayed in the gaily-coloured costume of the period' each measure 30 inches by 14 inches. They include Henry VIII, his six wives, Edward VI, Mary Tudor, Elizabeth I, Lady Jane Grey, Cardinal Wolsey, Mary Queen of Scots, Lord Darnley, James I of England and VI of Scotland, and Charles I as a boy. The portraits sold as one lot for £500, the Lancashire County Council stepping in to buy them and ensure that they were not removed.

It was Charles Scarisbrick in the nineteenth century who engaged the services of the elder Pugin to create a much grander dwelling than had housed earlier generations of the Scarisbrick family. Charles was reputedly 'the richest commoner in England.' From his travels on the Continent, he acquired carvings and statues with which to furnish the Hall. Pugin skilfully arranged a whole series of biblical and ecclesiastical carvings in the Oak Room. The Flood, David and Goliath, the Holy Spirit descending as a dove on Jesus, the Resurrection, and the Last Judgement are just some of the outstanding examples of Flemish wood-carving that fill the room.

The heavy oak door into the Great Hall enables one to go through from the Oak Room and view the 'Crowning of Thorns', twenty-four feet high and nine feet six inches wide – described in the sale catalogue as 'a Very Rare, Magnificent and Awe-Inspiring Early XVII Century Oak Pieta Wood Carving, of great size and remarkable workmanship.' It is thought to have come from Antwerp Cathedral, and one is left wondering why the cathedral authorities allowed Charles Scarisbrick to buy it. Also, how bare the wall would be where it used to stand, and how would such a huge piece have been transported? The figure of Christ being mocked by the Roman soldiers is depicted in a flamboyant gothic canopied setting with baroque spiral pilasters garlanded with vines. £750 was paid for it in the auction, again with the stipulation that it should remain in its place, as it still does today.

Two large bronze statues once stood in the centre of lawns in front of the Hall. Charles Scarisbrick was present in the London auction rooms where the statues were for sale. Standing nearby was Queen Victoria's consort, Prince Albert, who remarked to a friend, 'How well they would look in front of Windsor Castle!' Mr Scarisbrick immediately said to his friend, 'They will look just as well in front of Scarisbrick Hall!' – and that is where they went.

A School in a Mansion

The story goes that when Charles had a presbytery built for the use of the priest who served in the Hall Chapel, he ordered a gap to be left in the garden wall that was being built. After his death, the reason became clear. He had directed that his body be carried to the grave in a straight line from the Hall, and it was found that the straight line went through this gap.

When Charles died in 1860, he reputedly left £3 million (equivalent to about £300 million today), a sum derived largely from the land values of an expanding Southport. His sister, Lady Ann, sought to outdo her brother in the design and décor of the Hall. Augustus Pugin died in 1852, and Lady Ann gave his son, Edward, at the age of eighteen, the opportunity to show his own skills. The Blue Drawing Room is probably the finest example of his work, with exquisite marquetry, stained glass, and a beautifully painted ceiling. The tower, standing 156 feet high, was also the work of Edward Pugin, directed by Lady Ann. It replaced a more modest clock tower, as depicted in a carved panel on the staircase in the west wing. The initials AS are very visible, not only on the tower but also many times within the internal décor. Lady Ann Scarisbrick and Edward Pugin are depicted in large stained glass windows on a staircase near the Blue Drawing Room.

In December 1867, the Right Hon. W. E. Gladstone MP, on a visit to Ormskirk and Southport, paid a visit to Scarisbrick Hall, spending the night there at Lady Ann's invitation. Edward Pugin organised red Bengal lights to illuminate the half-mile drive from the main road to the front of the Hall, where servants moved about on the roof, positioning fires artificially coloured red, green, blue, and white, to give the Hall and the tower an enchanted appearance. The frosty night created a thin film of ice on the lake, where the whole effect was beautifully reflected.

Charles and Muriel Oxley were fully aware that, in taking ownership of a Grade I listed building, there were strict limits as to what they could do. The trainee teachers before them had left the Hall in generally good condition, although there were pieces of oak tracery missing from above the fireplace in the Red Drawing Room. Nevertheless, if any redecoration was to happen, it was clearly better to do it before the school opened, so Muriel set about this side of the enterprise while Charles was busy recruiting staff, meeting parents, enrolling pupils, and ensuring that the school could begin to function in September 1964.

The Oxleys' children – Marcus, Michael, Daniel and Rachel – were all educated at Tower College, and Michael and Rachel would later transfer to the Scarisbrick Sixth Form to do their A-levels. At the time when Charles and Muriel were planning to set up Scarisbrick Hall as a boarding school for boys, they took their four offspring to have a look round the premises. Rachel was still in the Junior School at Tower College and had already read enough of Enid Blyton's Malory Towers stories to envisage what boarding school life might be like. She was disappointed to find that Scarisbrick Hall would be a boarding school for boys only. When the family explored the Scarisbrick gymnasium, Rachel climbed up the wall bars and managed to get stuck, prompting her father to remark, 'Well, we'll have to buy the place now!'

It was important to secure good press coverage to get the message out about the new school. Charles Oxley knew that a good newspaper story was worth far more than expensive advertising, so the press near and far were alerted to the purchase. 'Mansion as Boys' School', 'Stately Home Will Be Preserved', and 'Scarisbrick Hall becomes Boys' Boarding School' were some of the newspaper headlines.

CHAPTER 2
THE EARLY YEARS

First of many pupils

The first pupil to be enrolled was Christopher Parry-Davies, whose father wrote twenty-five years later about the experience of his first meeting with Charles Oxley. His words appeared in *White Gates*, the magazine of the Old Students' Association, early in 1989, and as he wrote so eloquently of other events in 1964 as well as that first encounter, there is good reason to reproduce here the article written by Lt. Colonel David Parry-Davies:

JUSTUM ET TANACEM PROPOSITI VIRUM
(A man upright and strong in purpose)

Some twenty-five years ago I met Charles Oxley, a momentous year, for it was the year the Roman Catholic Church exonerated the Jews for the crucifixion of Jesus. The Olympics were held in Tokyo; Malta became independent; Martin Luther King was awarded the Nobel Peace Prize; the USA launched, successfully, the Saturn rocket; and France and Britain agreed to build a Channel Tunnel. In addition Mods and Rockers battled, spilling blood, on our beaches; Churchill left the Commons for the last time; and Dorothy Hodgkin was given the Nobel

Prize for Chemistry (the first woman to be awarded it). Scarisbrick Hall became a School for Boys.

When I first met Charles Oxley, Scarisbrick Hall was an empty shell, not yet recovered from producing varied potential mentors for, in its widest sense, the Field of Education. I stood in a bare, well-worn, dirty room just off the main corridor, resting against a very cold radiator, gazing through a clouded window onto an unkempt driveway, neglected fences and pastures, and a weed-choked lake. I pondered upon the events that had led me to this place: my meeting with a former companion of Lady Scarisbrick. My son, Christopher, at this time was in his last term at Seascale Preparatory School. We were anxious that his further education should be at a school with strong Christian ideals.

The Ghosts of Scarisbrick Hall were about me. The door opened and a tall, dark man stood there. The diary tells me that the first impressions were: an athlete, a surgeon, an Elizabethan actor awaiting his cue, a well-tried Service man. To my aid came the words of Psalm 35: "Take hold of shield and buckler, and stand..." Charles Oxley advanced with a boyish, disarming smile. "You must be..." adding, reading my thoughts, "This place will become charged with life."

We talked of desolate places both of us had known, men, boys, responsibilities of parents. It became a privilege to share his vision. Listening, I imagined I heard laughter, music, and boys' voices calling. I could sense movement; thought of the moon reflecting on the lake.

wisdom and established by understanding. We pray for all who teach and study here, all who work and worship here, that they may all be taught by Thee and see wondrous things out of Thy law. Especially do we pray that by Thy Spirit's guidance they may attain the all-surpassing knowledge of Thy truth through Him who is Himself the Truth, Thy Word and Thy Wisdom incarnate in human life, Jesus Christ our Lord. And this we ask, with thanksgiving, for His sake. Amen.

In a boarding school, the quality of the resident staff is of prime importance; in a new school, even more so, as they set standards and – perhaps unwittingly – initiate traditions that others will strive to follow. In David Riach and Ian Wride, Scarisbrick Hall School had two men who were willing to give time and attention to new boarders in a new school. Non-resident staff such as Mike Beilby, Ken Walker, Tudor Morris, and Barry Porter also provided extra-curricular activities to ensure that the boys had no need to be bored in their out-of-school hours. (Mike Beilby stands out in the earliest staff photograph as the gentle giant alluded to by former pupils who remember him. He made himself known to this writer in December 2023, still living in Southport with his wife.) Within a year or two, Reg Jones had arrived to introduce pottery and staffroom puns (he was a friend of Ken Dodd and had written jokes for the man from Knotty Ash), and Geoff Roberts, winner of the 1951 British Amateur Golf Championship, was sharing his skills with the boys, as well as teaching French.

Mr Oxley also came up with an idea, following a Fire Brigade inspection at the school. He suggested to the Chief Fire Officer at Southport Fire Station that a group of senior pupils start a Fire Cadet Corps. He had served with the Fire Service in Glasgow during the Second World War, so he knew the value of having people alert to the dangers of fire and knowing what to do in an emergency. The Chief Fire Officer responded to the suggestion by drawing up an eighteen-week syllabus of weekly meetings on a Monday evening. The boys who joined up were fascinated to visit the Fire Station and see how it worked. Alarm calls were a welcome intrusion into their course, providing the chance to observe the professionals at work. Within the first month of the course, a fire at a firelighter factory in Southport led the officer in charge to radio back to the station for the boys to go to the fire for on-the-spot instruction. This adventure merited a mention in the *Southport Visiter.*

Charles Oxley had a rugby background, both from his own school days and from the fact that Tower College was situated among the great Rugby League towns of St Helens, Warrington and Widnes. 'Rugger' was also the main winter game in grammar schools and public schools, and Charles had hopes of mixing it with these bastions of elitism not only academically but also on the sports field. Scarisbrick, however, lies in football country. In 1964 Southport FC – just four miles away - were still members of the Football League, and the bigger clubs – Liverpool, Everton, Preston North End, Bolton Wanderers, and the two Manchesters – drew far more support from the boys of Scarisbrick Hall School than any rugby team. In a short time, the school accepted the inevitable and swapped to football.

Entry requirements
In the early years of the school, it would not have been possible to have enough pupils if a strict academic entry

standard had been applied. That would come later. There was an insert in the earliest version of the prospectus that stated that 'All intended pupils are required to satisfy the entrance requirements

> either (a) by passing a test in English and Arithmetic which is held each Saturday morning between 9.30 and 12.30,
> or (b) by submitting evidence of a satisfactory standard of attainment, such as a headmaster's letter or one or two recent school reports.'

It is impossible to know how strictly these requirements were applied. What is undeniably the case is that some boys were admitted in the first intakes who really did not fit into the Oxley template in either academic standard or behaviour. We read, for example, in the Headmaster's newsletter to parents in April 1966, by which time the numbers had risen to 230, that entrance standards had been raised and that 'we have officially requested the withdrawal of several pupils, both boarders and day boys, because of their unsuitability.' Further on in the same letter, he writes that 'some boys' deportment needs improvement,' but that 'in general the task of consolidation is progressing well, but we will not be satisfied until we have a school worthy of the highest reputation.'

Peter Gregory, one of the earliest boarders, recalls how he came to be enrolled. His father worked in the Diplomatic Service and was posted to Tripoli, Libya, in the early 1960s, with 'boarding school' increasingly cropping up in conversations. It was during leave in the UK and a brief holiday in Blackpool that Mr and Mrs Gregory took Peter on a

'Mystery Tour' that passed through Ormskirk on the way to Southport. The coach driver's commentary included the information, as the coach passed the long wall of the Scarisbrick estate, that the Hall had just opened as a boys' boarding school. Peter noticed, out of the corner of his eye, that his father was making notes. A phone call the next day led to a visit the day after, and within an hour of first seeing the Hall, Peter was enrolled to start in January 1965, the school's second term.

The Headmaster's newsletter to parents in January 1965 expressed the sentiment that 'we ended our first term with a feeling of thankfulness that everything had gone so well.' There was mention of a badminton club, a Christian Fellowship, a choir, a motor club, a musical evening, fireworks on Bonfire Night and a trip to Blackpool illuminations.

Fees and flexible policies
That newsletter also gave an indication of how Charles and Muriel Oxley's policies were still in the formative stage, as it was of course his first experience of running his own boarding school. His experience at Victoria College in Egypt no doubt came in very useful. The Burnham Committee, who set teachers' salaries nationally, were to become a constant source of financial challenge to Charles and Muriel through the years, particularly when salary increases were – as often – backdated. The Oxleys liked to know in advance what their budget limits were likely to be, and Charles stated that it would be their policy 'always to give a full term's notice of any increase in fees as it is my policy to pay teaching staff in accordance with the Burnham Scale.' It was with some regret, therefore, that he had to announce a £2 per term increase in fees in the summer term!

Boarders' fees were initially set at £100 per term for nine- to twelve-year-olds, and £120 per term for thirteen- to nineteen-year-olds. Day boys' fees were just £30 per term. There were reductions for siblings, and also for the children of missionaries or full-time church workers. Lunches for day boys were charged at 12/6 per week (62p) and mid-morning milk was provided free, as in state schools.

Tom Brown's Schooldays, Just William, and Frank Richards' stories of Billy Bunter will have given some boys ideas both of what boarding school might be like, and also of ways to try to circumvent rules and authority. Alistair Telfer, one of the first intake in September 1964, had been bullied at prep school, so Scarisbrick offered a fresh start. 'We spent a lot of time exploring and seemed to be able to go to most places. To a nine-year-old it was an amazing place. Great palatial rooms with carvings, the Great Hall gallery with rows of cased stuffed birds. In the grounds, acres of woodland to build dens and tree houses.' Out in the woods behind the Hall was an ice-house, 'a popular place to play', and part-way along the back drive stood the mysterious mausoleum, only rarely investigated by intrepid boarders.

Where First School classroom blocks now stand there were greenhouses with vines, and 'a giant iron orangery which had frogs and newts in the stone water tanks... The one place totally out of bounds was the tower.' In later years the caretaker could be persuaded to allow departing Sixth-Formers to risk the perilous ascent up the narrow winding stairs, provided they gave an undertaking that the school would not be held responsible for any accident they might sustain. The views from near the top of the tower amply repaid their endeavours.

As the numbers of pupils increased, it became possible to apply entry requirements more stringently. The Maths and

English papers set and marked by Charles Oxley made no allowance for the gradual erosion nationally of the formal teaching methods he approved of. A boy who guessed that the plural of 'potato' might be 'chips' scored no marks for either grammar or ingenuity.

In May 1966 Mr Oxley wrote to parents whose sons had failed the Senior School Entrance Examination. Forty-four out of eighty candidates had passed, and the exam produced a marks range of 3% up to 97%. The letter explained that the school would be preparing pupils over seven years for GCE A-levels, including Latin, French, and separate sciences from the age of eleven. 'We want to know whether the candidate:

- has reached a sufficiently high standard to be ready to start the course;
- has the mental ability to assimilate knowledge, to acquire linguistic and mathematical skills and to understand and correlate processes;
- has power to concentrate, eagerness to learn and has a developing self-discipline sufficient to make himself persevere with subjects which hold no special interest for him;
- and will have the constant support and encouragement from home to help him see the course through to a successful conclusion.

'It is fairly easy to answer (a) but the other factors are largely unknown, and although we are aware of them, we must decide mainly on the child's present standard of attainment.'

Mr Oxley was honest enough in that final sentence to admit that his testing process was hardly an exact science, but there had to be some way of finding out what a boy had learnt and could do.

In less than two years from the school's opening, Scarisbrick Hall had made sufficient impact on public awareness to merit a visit from *Lancashire Life*. That popular magazine produced a three-page spread with nine photographs and a very sympathetic article in its July issue in 1966.

Facilities for boarders? 'No depressing dormitories with serried rows of beds, but charmingly decorated bedrooms – the biggest have four beds in them, but most of them have just one or two – no shabby common rooms, but beautiful rooms with chairs and couches delightfully covered in good, modern fabrics. In this respect the place has more the feeling of a well-run private hotel than a school.' The reporter evidently did not visit on a cold winter evening when boarders clutched hot water bottles to their chests or curried favour with the chef so as to be able to sit on a hot-plate to keep warm!

The article referred to 'a happy staff of men all excellently qualified and all really interested in the boys' extra-curricular, as well as classroom activities.' Strictly speaking, though, the staff were not exclusively male: teachers and pupils from that era recall, for example, Susan Ledson not only as a young female teacher, but also formidably driving a farm tractor up and down the kitchen garden to prepare the ground for building operations. (Vincent's Nurseries had previously used the land for growing their plants.)

Alternative to comprehensive schools
The official introduction of comprehensive schools as the national norm in 1965 led many parents familiar with grammar schools to look outside the state system for the first

time. The long-established independent schools nearest geographically to Scarisbrick Hall were St Mary's and Merchant Taylors', both in Crosby, and Liverpool College. However, families living in the area of Wigan, Standish, and Parbold, who might look east towards Bolton School, could now avail themselves of coach transport specially provided to and from Scarisbrick. Coaches also served Crosby, Maghull, Formby and Southport, thereby offering a local challenge to the older schools.

In his Speech Day report in 1967, Charles Oxley was able to announce that the school numbers had almost reached 300, with 115 boarders and 183 day boys. The Junior School had one form each of eight-, nine-, and ten-year-olds, while there were two forms in each of the Senior School year groups plus a Lower Sixth of seventeen, including three girls.

'Two generous donations' had been received from a Christian businessman to improve amenities. Fees covered the general running of the school, but not capital expenditure on, for example, new classroom blocks. Mr and Mrs Oxley had installed new boilers at a cost of £2,300; the lake had been cleared of weeds; land had been prepared in the old kitchen garden area for a new classroom block; a twelve-seater minibus had been ordered. New toilets had been fitted out in the courtyard: 'We did not arrange an official opening ceremony, but a small boy in Lower School in a private ceremony unofficially but effectively did the job as soon as the plumbers left!'

The Department of Education and Science had sent a team of eight inspectors to cast their eyes over the fledgling school and had granted 'provisional recognition'; this was important as the Labour government of the day was making noises about requiring all independent schools to become 'recognised' or to close down.

Parents' assistance

Mr Oxley was never one for having parents popping in and out of school unannounced; if they needed to see him, they should ring for an appointment. The ideal parents were the ones who paid the fees promptly and made sure that their child arrived on time, smartly dressed in school uniform and ready to work hard. Attempts by some parents over the years to have a say in the running of the school – perhaps as governors – were always rejected. Nonetheless, he did not object when a group of parents offered to form a small committee to raise the funds for an all-weather cricket pitch. And he positively encouraged parents to do all they could to increase the number and quality of books in the school library. Over 100 parents contributed to the installation of the cricket pitch, which enabled school teams to play in the Southport Schools Leagues.

Mystery surrounds the acquisition of a wooden construction that suddenly appeared behind the Hall. It may have been picked up at a bargain price from another school, but it was swiftly erected and wired for electricity for use as both a geography room and careers room. Barry Porter was in charge of both. Ian Wride also ran a tuckshop there, raising funds for War on Want. The glorified shed did not last long. One night it caught fire and was well ablaze before any boarding staff or pupils realised. Day staff and boys arriving the next day blinked when they saw the smouldering timbers and piles of ash. The mystery of the burnt-out geography room at least afforded opportunities for pupils' creative writing. Was it the ghost of Lady Ann Scarisbrick objecting to an old shed stuck in the grounds of her beloved Hall? Surely it was not a result of boarders slipping in for a crafty cigarette or a midnight party? The true cause of the fire remains a mystery. And surely any place with a history needs an element of mystery?

Rules for everybody
Although he was regarded as a strict disciplinarian, Mr Oxley was prepared to adapt his initial policies and regulations in the light of experience. He had imposed the arbitrary requirement on boys to wear a school cap until they attained the height of five feet ten inches. It took several years of persuasion for him to recognise that, even in the Sixth Form, some boys would never reach that height, and so, eventually, he changed the rule.

In order to preserve the quality and colour of the mosaic floors in the main corridor and Great Hall, all boys had to wear traditional-style brown sandals indoors, changing to black leather shoes for outdoor wear. However, as the school expanded and classroom blocks were built behind the main Hall, it became accepted that black shoes should be standard uniform at all times.

By 1968, with numbers still growing and standards rising, Mr Oxley felt the time was right to set down in some detail exactly how he wanted his school to operate. He published three booklets, *Pupils' Guide, Parents' Guide* and *Staff Handbook*.

Pupils were encouraged to 'Make up your mind from the start that you are going to enjoy life at Scarisbrick Hall. Make friends with at least two pupils and join in as many school activities as you can.

'Remember that the more you put into school, the more you will get out of it. This is true of anything worthwhile – your education, your job, your hobbies, your faith and your life.'

Offences that would incur the wrath of the staff included the usual bullying, smoking, insolence to staff members and persistent disobedience, but also 'careless disregard for your own property, including clothing ... snobbishness ... and bad conduct out of school which reflects adversely on the reputation of the school.

'When addressed by a staff member, stand properly, not with hands in pockets. ... Address staff members in a respectful manner, using correct forms of address: "Sir" for masters and male visitors; lady staff members and non-teaching staff should be addressed by name, except the Matrons and the Chef, who should be addressed as "Matron" and "Chef". ... In the corridors or on the stairs, stand aside to allow staff members or visitors to pass. On meeting a staff member or visitor while wearing your cap, touch it politely.'

Boarders had to write a 'proper letter home each week.' Long before mobile phones appeared, the rule was that 'Boarders must not make or receive telephone calls at school without permission.' They had to attend a Sunday morning service, either at the local parish church, St Mark's, in the early days, or, later on, at a choice of local denominational churches. 'Boarders must not bring to school – exhibitionist clothing (*no indication as to how this was defined*), knives (except small penknives), matches, catapults, playing cards, or anything that is likely to cause a disturbance.' Transistor radios and comics, however, were acceptable for leisure time use.

Under 'Rules Regarding Written Work' came the following:

'Every piece of work – classwork or prep – must have a heading with a description of the work written on the left of the page, starting right at the margin. The date is put on the same line on the right of the page and in the following way only – 9.9.67. One line is left unused after the heading. A pencil line is drawn with a ruler under each completed exercise. ... Handwriting and figures must be neat and legible. The practice of "printing" some capital letters in a piece of handwriting is not allowed. Mis-spelt words must be written out so as to fill one line, unless the word was specifically set for learning, in which case it must fill three lines. When a "correction" is done wrongly, it must fill five lines. When words like "there" and "were" are confused with "their" and "where", three one-line sentences must be written for both words to show the correct meaning.'

The first edition of the *Staff Handbook* runs to twenty-two pages, outlining the school's constitution, doctrinal basis, staff organisation, staff meetings, daily routine with exact times given from 7.20 a.m. rising bell to 6.45 p.m. evening prayers, responsibilities of form masters, house masters, subject masters. Such tight prescriptions were thought to be necessary, partly because individual job descriptions did not appear at that time, but also because Mr Oxley divided his time between the two schools, Tower College and Scarisbrick Hall, and he did not want his absence to be a cause of vagueness or a vacuum in the running of the schools. He was trying to remove any potential areas of uncertainty from the minds of his teachers, but the final page of the *Staff Handbook* shows his awareness of a teacher's need for some flexibility in the fundamental area of teaching:

> *FINALLY... No two teachers have exactly the same approach, would use the same methods or the same things for special emphasis and it would not be a good thing if it were otherwise. A middle way has to be found between rigid uniformity in everything on the one hand and confusion and indiscipline on the other. Staff members who perhaps at times find the foregoing procedure irksome, can console themselves by the fact that they have full freedom*

where it really matters, viz. in the way in which they choose to plan their course and teach their subjects.

It is sincerely hoped that members of the teaching staff of Scarisbrick Hall will enjoy the sense of fulfilment and satisfaction which is the teacher's highest reward.

School magazines

The boarding side of school certainly had an international quality. Earliest editions of the school magazine include boys' accounts of life in Hong Kong, Zambia, South Africa, Singapore, Japan, Mongolia, Portugal, Kenya, Libya, Tanzania, and India. There are reports also of railway modellers, a pets club and of croquet on the lawn. Some of these activities achieved official status, with acronyms such as SLOSH (Small Livestock Owners of Scarisbrick Hall – presumably tall owners were also allowed in), SHIPS (Scarisbrick Hall Independent Pigeon Society – twenty pigeons, thirteen members, a waterproof loft), and SCRAM (SCarisbrick RAilway Modellers – sadly, the shed where they used to meet disappeared during one vacation, so the club did have to scram).

The school magazine also gave voice to individual opinions on matters of international and local importance. For example:

'Instead of sending food and clothing to the people of India, it would be better to send birth-control pills to stop the rapid increase in population.'
'The dock strike in Liverpool is appalling. Our luggage from Nigeria came to England and because of the strike it left Liverpool and went to Amsterdam.'
'Radio One is a plastic imitation of Radio Caroline.'

'School meals have become much better, but only the bigger boys get seconds.'

'I hope the Americans will crush Chairman Mao. If you can crush all the Communists the world will be better off.'

'The introduction of the breathalyser is a good thing.'

Peter Gregory recalls that from the beginning, life as a boarder was in some ways fairly Spartan, with few facilities, yet at the same time 'very much a family atmosphere in the evenings and especially at weekends.' That was largely down to the initiative and consideration of Messrs Riach, Wride and Harmer-Smith – the original resident teachers – together with the Matron and the Chef, plus of course Mr Oxley himself. Before any clubs began to take shape, and with neither library nor television in those very early days, it was a case of exploring the grounds on foot or by bicycle, with games of 'Pirates' in the gym and at the weekend compulsory walks with Matron. These walks were in addition to the walk to the local parish church, St Mark's, where during term time the congregation doubled in size and more than halved in average age.

Night-time could be testing time for the courage of a young boarder. Creaking floorboards, cavernous rooms, some bedrooms far from a bathroom, all converged in the mind of a boy needing the toilet in the middle of the darkness of night. Add to that the rumours of Lady Ann Scarisbrick's ghost appearing in the Hall and it was quite understandable that a boy would wake his room-mate to accompany him to the bathroom and back.

Television first appeared in the school on 30th January 1965 for the state funeral of Sir Winston Churchill; this was an old black and white set loaned by a parent and the boys sat on wooden benches until the set was removed immediately after the funeral. It was several months later that a permanent television appeared in the Boarders' Common Room for 'selected programmes only' and never on Sunday. Thursday evenings brought a regular highlight for lusty teenage boys: *Top of the Pops* not only kept them up to date with the latest hits, but also offered the sight of Pan's People, a group of nubile dancing girls in fairly skimpy outfits.

Stephen Bunce boarded from the age of just nine and, although he had an older brother with him, he still went through homesickness and some unhappiness caused by other pupils. 'I thoroughly enjoyed my time at school and am very grateful for the experience. I think the most enduring lesson I learnt was the value of people. I don't remember it being spoken, but the message I heard was just because your parents pay for your education doesn't make you better than anyone else.'

To some outsiders, however, the sight of a Scarisbrick Hall School uniform alighting from a coach somewhere in Southport or Crosby stirred an antagonism that could lead to unkind words or even physical bullying. A boy who had grown up with a bunch of mates who all went to the same local primary school now found himself ostracised for apparently being 'posh' and 'superior.' That was one of the hardest things for some children to cope with during their Scarisbrick years. Another was the Christian emphasis which, for some particularly with no church background, felt oppressive.

One School & Two Families

Scarisbrick Hall

The former teacher training college for sale 1963

The Early Years

Charles and Muriel Oxley

*The Oxley family:
(l to r) Marcus, Charles, Rachel, Muriel, Danny, Michael*

One School & Two Families

The three Greek words on the original blazer badge mean 'grace and knowledge' - taken from a Bible verse: 'But grow in the grace and knowledge of our Lord and Saviour Jesus Christ.' (2 Peter 3:18)

CHAPTER 3
EXPANSION INTO THE SEVENTIES

Staff changes

By the end of the 1960s, several new and additional staff had arrived. David Riach had been Senior Tutor and Senior Housemaster, but he did not fit the ideal that Mr Oxley was looking for in a Senior Tutor, which was someone with impressive qualifications, experience and also a clear commitment to the evangelical Christian faith. Peter Kimber did seem to match up to that ideal. He was himself a 'missionary's kid' who went through primary education in India before attending St Lawrence College, Ramsgate, which had its own evangelical ethos. After graduating from Oxford and time working in Antarctica, Peter spent four years teaching at Glasgow Academy, studying for an M Ed and getting married to Hilda. It was Hilda's parents who had a Brethren friend who knew of Charles Oxley and visited Scarisbrick. Their enthusiasm for the school's Christian ethos led to Peter making contact with Mr Oxley, and after a visit to the school he was invited to apply for the post of Senior Tutor, which he accepted when it was offered.

David Riach continued for another year as Senior Housemaster and then moved on. Peter Kimber arrived about a week before the school year began in September 1969 to find that one of his jobs was to work out a timetable from scratch. Mr Oxley presented him with what he called a 'spread of lessons', specifying which teacher had how many lessons with which classes. Beyond that, Peter could have been on his own, but it says much for the character and kindness of both David Riach and Ian Wride that they rallied round and gave Peter as much help as they could.

Among other well qualified and experienced staff who were joining the school about that time were several who were very open about their Christian faith and very keen to develop the spiritual life of the school. Geoffrey Charrett, in the Boarders' Fellowship, and John Sutton-Smith, through the lunch-time meetings of the Christian Fellowship, both made the teaching of the Christian faith relevant to young people. They and other members of staff took part in the regular rota of morning assemblies which normally included a hymn, a Bible reading and brief exposition, plus a prayer and the Lord's Prayer. As the school developed, there were roughly a third of the teaching staff who had a strong Christian faith, maybe another third who might be classed as nominal or cultural Christians, and others who perhaps felt that 'religion' was a totally private matter.

Charles and Muriel Oxley's minimum requirement from a member of staff was to be 'in sympathy' with the Christian stance of the school. Sadly, some of that sympathy ebbed away among some teachers who were upset by what seemed to them to be unduly harsh judgements of pupil misdemeanours, some of which led to exclusion from the school. Corporal punishment was still widely accepted in both state and independent schools at that time, so that the Headmaster, the Senior Housemaster and the Senior Tutor were in line with the times in applying the slipper to the seat of learning!

Andrew Wilcockson was one boarder who recalls being dealt with in this way for transgressions such as playing hide-and-seek after lights out or engaging in water fights in the

Expansion into the Seventies

bathrooms. 'I bear absolutely no grudges,' says Andrew; 'we knew well the risks and penalties, but at the time it no doubt seemed a good idea, and one didn't wish to appear *soft.* My father had said explicitly to Mr Oxley that if I needed caning he was to do so.' By the time Andrew himself became a teacher in an independent school, his views on corporal punishment had changed considerably.

Andrew and others also recall how boarders used to explore the purpose-built cellars and tunnels that spread out under the Hall building. Some cellars were used for storing either coal or boarders' luggage, but the tunnels were ideal for prompting boys' inquisitive nature. Bear in mind that the Hall itself, widely recognised as being constructed to the design of the Pugins in the nineteenth century, actually stood on the same ground as an earlier, Elizabethan house, and the tunnels may have been useful for ventilation purposes centuries ago. In the 1970s, however, they offered illicit entertainment. Andrew made his way along a tunnel one evening, saw a trap door above his head, pushed it up and emerged in the middle of a group of senior boys doing extra English with Mr Morris! The short, sharp punishment he later received for his trouble was probably worth it for the look on the faces of the group as he ascended from below.

Several former pupils have told of how these tunnels and trap doors came in useful for confusing an unwary teacher. A boy would disappear from a classroom as if by magic while the teacher was writing on the blackboard, only to reappear later in the lesson. One teacher who would never have been caught out in this way was Ivor Thomas, the History master from the earliest days of the school. He was well past 'normal' retirement age, but still teaching, when he had a heart attack. So dedicated was he to his A-level students' success that, while his recuperation prevented him from driving in to school, an arrangement was made for the four boys to be driven by one of their number over to Mr Thomas' home three times a week to complete their course.

School plays

By the time that Peter Kimber arrived in 1969, an Old Boys' Association had been set up; sixteen members had their inaugural dinner in the Great Hall. Also, Tudor Morris, the Head of English, persuaded two other staff members to help him produce a school play – *The Insect Play* by the brothers Capek.

Drama was never included in those days as a discrete subject in the Scarisbrick Hall curriculum. Yet, in putting on a production, everyone could see the benefits of teamwork, voice projection, set design and building, plus the individual character development of dozens of pupils. One boy, who had a very noticeable stammer in normal conversation, surprised everyone when he turned up for an audition for a school play. Once he stood on the stage, his stammer disappeared completely and he took on very successfully a major role in Shaw's *Arms and the Man*.

Tudor Morris' initiative with school plays was matched by his project to transform the boathouse into a theatre. As a post-GCE activity in the latter part of the summer term, he organised a team of boys to clear away debris, replace missing planks, decorate and make the boathouse by the weir serviceable for a play, which the boys themselves performed to a necessarily small but appreciative audience.

The lake itself, when the school first began, was full of weeds and it took a real effort to clear them away. In later years, the lake was totally drained to allow dredging machines to go down to the bed of the lake and remove hundreds of tons of silt. The cost of the operation, which lasted several weeks, was offset by local farmers taking the silt to spread on their fields. This process served as a reminder that much farmland in the Scarisbrick township was reclaimed from the original Martin Mere.

ISA Membership

The Department for Education and Science conducted a full inspection in March 1970. The report recognised that the school was still very young and that resources took time to accumulate. Areas in need of development included science storage space, audio-visual equipment, closer collaboration between the Senior and Junior schools, more continuity in the teaching of Geography and Maths. French was taught from a grammar base, with lots of translation, and 'a lighter approach to the language requires to be introduced.' The Music department was 'beginning to flourish.' The overall verdict of the inspectors was this: 'The atmosphere and environment of Scarisbrick Hall School is honest and straightforward, the relations between staff and pupils are relaxed but hardworking, and the community is a friendly and educative one.'

Scarisbrick Hall School became a member of the Independent Schools Association, which, along with other groupings such as the Headmasters' Conference, the Girls' Schools Association, the Society of Headmasters of Independent Schools and the Independent Association of Prep Schools, represented the large majority of independent schools across the country. The ISA comprised over 300 schools and each region held competitions in athletics, swimming, cross country and drama, as well as representing member schools in the Independent Schools Council.

It became a high point of the Scarisbrick sporting calendar for boys to compete in the ISA North-West Athletics Championships, held at Stretford in Manchester. To win an event there meant that you went on to represent the North-West in the National ISA Championships, initially at Oxford, later at Birmingham. In July 1969, in the North-West event, Scarisbrick's senior boys came first overall and the juniors second. Sixteen individual champions went from Scarisbrick to represent the North-West at Oxford, where eight became National ISA champions, helping the North-West team to first place among the regions. Success on this scale became the norm for the school.

The ISA also played its part in defending the rights of parents to choose independent schools for their children. From time to time political pressure would be applied, particularly from a Labour government, to try and get rid of independent schools. Charles Oxley urged parents to attend an ISA rally in October 1969 at Belle Vue, Manchester, on the theme of 'Freedom of choice in Education', as well as suggesting that they write letters to MPs whenever the threat re-emerged.

Charles and Muriel Oxley knew that for the school to succeed educationally it had to have financial stability. In order to buy Scarisbrick Hall in 1963, they took out a banker's loan of £21,000, which they were able to pay off in seven years, thanks in part to the wedding photography which Muriel still undertook for several years while still helping to run the two schools. In his letter to parents in November 1969, Mr Oxley included a section on finance:

'All the money received in termly fees and other charges has been spent on the cost of running the school and on improving the amenities of the school. The Company does not make a profit for any shareholders and for the first four years my wife and I have not drawn any salary. My wife and I bought the premises and neither the capital nor the interest has been charged to the Company. The Company has been given a fifty-year lease on the property at a nominal rent which has not been drawn from the Company.

'The School received two gifts of £5,000 each from a Christian friend of mine and about £1,500 from various parents. In consequence, we have been able to spend thousands of pounds on the amenities of the school towards which the termly fees have contributed a very small fraction.'

Girls admitted
Because of its sixth form, Scarisbrick Hall was an attractive proposition for pupils from Tower College whose parents wanted to maintain the Oxley connection. Even in the late 1960s a couple of girls were admitted for their A Levels. Moreover, parents who had sons at Scarisbrick and daughters elsewhere kept asking Mr Oxley whether he would consider admitting girls as well. By the time Trinity Hall, a Methodist girls' school in Southport, closed in 1970, the pressure became irresistible. In that year, Scarisbrick Hall became a mixed school for day boys and girls and a boarding school for boys; it would not be long, however, before girls were also able to board. Weekly boarding was always available for those who wanted their children home for the weekend and at school from Monday to Friday. Some Tower College students joined the Scarisbrick Sixth Form as weekly boarders.

It was the boarding element of the school that had led Mr Oxley from the start to extend the school day until 5.45 p.m., with prep – also known as homework – taken at school under supervision. However, as the numbers in the Junior School increased, and later a Kindergarten was added, the day was simply too long for many young children. Arrangements were made for them to be picked up at 4.00 or 4.30 p.m., but that in turn inconvenienced families with children in both Seniors and Juniors who understandably wanted to be able to take them home at the same time. Eventually, prep at school for day pupils was dropped and the school day officially ended at 4.00 for the Junior and Kindergarten classes and 4.15 for the Seniors.

In 1970 the decision was taken to convert the school boilers from coal to oil at a cost of £2,500. Rather less expensive was a week's ski holiday in the Christmas holidays – flights, accommodation, hire of equipment and six days' ski tuition, all for £60! Skiing holidays were one of several initiatives of Peter Kimber.

At Speech Day in October 1971 the Headmaster reported that the total of 366 pupils included 58 girls – 'nearly twice as many as last year. This is better than we expected and the girls themselves are better than some of us expected.' This last remark of Mr Oxley's aimed to counter the reservations that some staff members had when it was mooted that girls would be admitted. Some teachers had themselves been educated at boys' grammar schools and came to Scarisbrick to teach boys. Suddenly, creatures in pinafore dresses and skirts began to appear, and any 'all lads together' approaches to lessons had to be modified or discarded. Some feared the presence of the opposite sex would prove a distraction to teenage boys, but what happened was that academically it was the girls who usually set the pace and socially they quickly cut down to size any boy who was foolish enough to try and show off in front of the girls.

Charles and Muriel Oxley were determined to avoid any pairing off between the sexes, so they made it a rule that a boy and girl who had taken a fancy to each other should not hold hands and that other people should be present when a couple were together. Suffice it to say that several couples emerged from schooldays with their relationship intact, and indeed a number of marriages resulted from relationships that began at school.

Eastern intake
1971 not only saw girls arriving but was also the year when pupils started to join the school from the Far East. Three Malaysian and two Chinese students were initially admitted as Sixth Form boarders. It is known that a British police inspector went out to work in the Hong Kong police and left his sons boarding at Scarisbrick. So impressed was this officer with his sons' education that he seems to have recommended Scarisbrick Hall School to most if not all of the police officers in Hong Kong. Year after year, applications came in and Chinese boarders were admitted. Unfortunately, assurances from Hong Kong about the standard of English of these applicants proved to be less than reliable, so much so that remedial work was needed if the boys were going to understand the various subjects being taught in English.

Archimedes' principle about the displacement of water also seems to have been missing from the Hong Kong physics syllabus, as one rather large student, Raymond Chin, placed himself in a very full bath, eliciting cries other than 'Eureka!' from the staff-room immediately below as the bath water dripped through the ceiling.

The newsletter dated 31st December 1971 gives the reasons why a fees increase would be needed in the Summer Term 1972. Teachers' salaries had increased by 'more than the 10% expected.' Costs had also risen for food, fuel oil, books, printing and postage. Maintenance and repairs included resurfacing the front drive, improved lighting at the front and rear of the main Hall, fire alarms overhauled, smoke detectors installed, metal window frames in eight new wing dormitories replaced, and new classrooms and several bedrooms redecorated.

Holidays in term-time
With the number of boarders now approaching 120, some tightening up was needed. Several boarders arrived at the start of term with large amounts of pocket money, others with none. Mr Oxley's recommendation was a sum of £4 or £5. Also, travel arrangements had become sloppy, with some pupils leaving before the end of term or arriving after the new term had begun. Parents were presenting the school with a fait accompli by getting airlines to send flight tickets directly to school at short notice, with no prior warning from home. In future, the newsletter stated, travelling must take place within the official holiday period. Only in exceptional circumstances would permission be given for a boarder to arrive late or leave early.

Boarders had some interesting characters to cope with among resident staff. There could scarcely have been a bigger contrast, for example, between Bob Freak, a scholarly, Christian, gentle man who had been a missionary headmaster in Uganda (until Idi Amin made life very tough), and Brian Hodgkins, reportedly from a military background, who seemed to delight in having fire drills at unearthly hours and dishing out punishments like confetti.

The school had generous holidays of almost three weeks at Christmas and Easter, and seven weeks in the summer, plus half-term breaks of a full week each. The Christmas and Easter vacations allowed all boarders to have a reasonable amount of time at home, even in the case of one family whose parents lived in the Solomon Islands, where a homeward journey could take two full days.

The problem of holidays encroaching on term-time was not confined to boarders, however. Forty years before state school heads began to be able to impose fines on parents who took children away on holiday in term-time, Charles Oxley had had enough of the same problem and wrote to parents accordingly: 'Children whose parents take them off on holiday during term-time or steal extra days at the beginning and end of term, have to leave and their places will be given to pupils who will put in proper attendance.' He backed up this warning with action on more than one occasion.

By 1972-73 the school had 460 pupils, of whom 130 were boarders. There were four classes in the Junior School and a three-form entry into the Seniors, with forty students in the Sixth Form. That year also marked the first admission of Scarisbrick Hall students to Oxford University. Daniel Hastings, Roger Knight and Andrew Scott all gained entry to St Peter's College, where Peter Kimber had been a student. Peter's letter of recommendation to the College may have assisted the three boys' admission, but they proved to be well worthy of a place at Oxford. Andrew was awarded the Law Prize for his year and went on to be described as 'the best tax lawyer in Europe.' Daniel became a Professor of Engineering at the Massachusetts Institute of Technology, one of the world's outstanding universities.

Changes at the top
That was to be Peter Kimber's swansong. He had observed Charles Oxley's way of running the school and, although there

was much that he approved of, there were areas where he tried to bring about change, but met strong resistance. The personal relationship between the two men was important. The differences sadly came to a head half-way through Peter Kimber's third year at Scarisbrick, when Charles Oxley said to him, 'This isn't working. I think you need to find another job.' This was not the sack as such, but it was clear that Peter did not have a long-term future at the school. After his fourth year at Scarisbrick Hall he made the move back to Scotland with his wife and two small sons, and began working for the Scottish Examinations Board.

Peter Kimber's replacement was the present writer. I had joined the staff in September 1968 in the English department and became Head of English when Tudor Morris departed the following year. My previous teaching experience was at Kingswood School in Bath, a Methodist boys' boarding school founded by John Wesley. I had been a small cog in a large and well-oiled machine there, whereas Scarisbrick Hall represented a fresh challenge: a school only four years old when I arrived appealed to some kind of pioneering spirit in me. As head of department I had some responsibility but my time was still mostly spent in the classroom, which is where I was happiest. When Mr Oxley approached me about following Peter Kimber, I had some reservations. I had seen the potential if those two men could have formed a team, but the very strength of personality of both men made it almost inevitable that division would come. Nevertheless, I came to the point where I felt that I should say Yes to Mr and Mrs Oxley and I was appointed Deputy Head from September 1973.

By this time, the Fifth Form pupils were achieving an average of 4.4 subject passes each at GCE Ordinary Level, which was quite pleasing in itself but led Mr Oxley to declare that he would not be satisfied until the average was six subject passes.

Political battle-ground
Independent schools were again under attack from the Labour Party. When Roy (later Lord) Hattersley MP openly stated that he hoped to see the abolition of all independent schools before he died, Charles Oxley's response was: 'Long may he live!'

He recognised that there were powerful forces at work in reshaping the state's provision of education in schools. His judgement was clear and unequivocal: 'Non-selective, non-streamed secondary schooling spells non-sense educationally.' In practical terms, it would be a huge logistical task to transfer the 7% of privately-educated children into state schools. He was scathing about 'play-way methods in many primary schools' and the abolition of the 11+ which he saw as lowering the standard of attainment in basic subjects in many state schools. He was in no doubt that it was impossible to provide for the needs of very bright children and slow children in one class. Even to have graded groups around their own tables displeased him, as many of the pupils would have their backs to the teacher and the blackboard. Each pupil should have his or her own desk and be seated in straight lines facing teacher and blackboard.

To Mr Hattersley's talk of 'the privileged few' who attended independent schools, Mr Oxley responded: 'The parents who send their children to independent schools are not buying a privilege, they are exercising a right – a fundamental human right to spend their money in any lawful way they choose. School fees are paid out of taxed income after the contribution to the state system has been paid. ... The nationalisation of education will solve no problems and will create many more.'

He would have had strong words to say to a Labour government in 2024 that imposed a 20% value added tax on independent school fees.

Mr Oxley also had reservations from a spiritual perspective about what was happening. He was appalled when a leading representative of the British Humanist Association – an atheist – was appointed to the Religious Education Council. 'Many children are sent to Scarisbrick and to our associated school, Tower College,' he wrote to parents, 'because of its Christian character and aims and that the education is based on the Christian faith. There are very powerful influences at work in the state school system to eliminate any Christian or religious influence. If independent schools are abolished, parents have no choice but to send their children to schools where they do not know who is feeding their child's mind or with what. They could well be subject to humanistic, atheistic and anarchic influences. It is up to parents therefore to defend their right to freedom of choice in education. It is our job at school to see that you have something worth fighting for.'

CHAPTER 4

TEN YEARS ON

1974 marked the ten-year anniversary of the opening of the school and Mr Oxley's Speech Day report reviewed the whole decade.

- Pupil numbers had risen from 71 to 484.
- Boarding numbers had risen from twenty-three to 130, including twelve girls.
- The Sixth Form had sixty students, sixteen in the Upper Sixth and forty-four in the Lower Sixth.
- From two full-time and five part-time teachers, the staff now comprised twenty full-time and ten part-time teachers, equivalent to twenty-six full-time.
- Coaches transporting pupils to and from school had increased from one to six.
- The school had acquired its own thirty-seven-seater coach, 'slightly second-hand but with all its certificates of fitness. So if you should see me driving the coach proudly wearing my PSV badge, wave smartly and keep well out of the way.'
- Nineteen new classrooms built and the engine house converted to a pottery room.
- A new science teaching block almost completed. This was designed by Geoffrey Charrett, the Head of Science, and contained laboratories for physics, chemistry,

biology, general science and geography, plus a prep room and an audio-visual room.

Following the sad death of Mrs Dutton, the Head of the Junior School, through protracted illness, Miss Valerie Wright had been appointed acting Head of Juniors. She quickly established herself as a capable, conscientious lady who was to lead the Junior School for the next twenty years before serious illness also claimed her.

Mr Oxley's address also made comment on declining standards in attainment as measured by the Senior School Entrance Examination. No longer could he include questions about parts of speech, as the candidates clearly did not even understand such a question. Light relief for the exam marker came with occasional flashes of insight, however. 'Queen Elizabeth was the best king England ever had' and 'Enoch Powell was the founder of the Brownies' were two contributions, but they were undoubtedly outshone by the lad who, when asked to work out the age of a man born in 1925, scrawled many calculations that made no sense to the marker, then crossed them all out and wrote 'This man was never born.'

Surveys at that time always showed a vast majority of parents in favour of standards and values based on the Judaeo-Christian tradition, whether or not they identified themselves as Christians. At a conference on morning assemblies, Charles Oxley had listened to a delegate describing a comprehensive school 'not a hundred miles from here', where the Head was an atheist, there was no morning assembly and the lower end of the school had no Scripture lessons because there was only one staff member out of over 100 prepared to teach the subject. The walls of the Sixth Form Common Room were covered with posters of Chairman Mao.

Christian standards

By contrast, Scarisbrick Hall School was very clear in having morning assembly every day led by committed Christian teachers; Scripture taught in the main-stream curriculum; and voluntary Christian groups meeting at lunch-time to meet the needs of those wanting to know more about the Christian faith. Over the next twenty years, the notion of 'Scripture' as a discrete subject – already regarded by many as anachronistic – took on various guises: Religious Knowledge, Religious Education, Religious Studies. GCE Ordinary and Advanced Level courses which had focused on sections of the Old and New Testaments gradually lost their clear biblical priority and began to introduce texts of other religions. At Scarisbrick, the preference was to teach biblical Christianity up to and including 'O' Level, with other religions included in the General Studies course in the Sixth Form.

As Charles Oxley saw the erosion of the Christian emphasis from syllabuses, he tried to gain support from church leaders and Bible College heads for an Examination Board for Biblical and Religious Studies, which he hoped would gain acceptance as an authentic alternative to the increasingly non-biblical 'O' and A-level qualifications. As he had also been involved in setting up Liverpool Bible College, he proposed that the EBBRS would also produce courses leading to higher-level certificates and diplomas. His bulwark against the eroding tides, however, never gained the widespread acceptance it needed.

This particular battle-ground was just one of many in which Charles Oxley played a prominent role, as he observed society turning away from Judaeo-Christian traditions and values. If a campaign group did not exist, he founded one, either locally or further afield. He was a strong supporter of the Nationwide Festival of Light, a campaign led by Malcolm Muggeridge, Lord

Longford, Mary Whitehouse and various church leaders to counter the increasingly 'permissive society' in Britain in the 1960s and early 1970s. He went on to work closely with Mrs Whitehouse in her crusade to clean up television, which became the National Viewers and Listeners Association. It was in that context that Charles set up a project with Scarisbrick Hall boarders that was to achieve national press coverage and set one young man on course for a highly influential career.

The Hastings Report
Michael Hastings was a boarder along with his older brother Daniel. Both had attended Tower College as Juniors before the family moved to Jamaica. Such was their parents' high regard for the Oxleys and their schools that they sent the boys to Scarisbrick six years later to complete their schooling.

Whereas Daniel went on to scale the academic heights via Oxford University and a professorial chair at the Massachusetts Institute of Technology, Michael managed just two A-level passes and a 2:2 degree in Theology. What he did have, however, was a strong sense of public service and a determination to do all within his power to improve the lot of disadvantaged people and nations. After a short time as an R.E teacher, he would move into government service, then into television as GMTV's chief political correspondent. At the BBC he began as presenter of *Around Westminster* before becoming Head of Public Affairs and then the first Head of Corporate Social Responsibility in 2003. He has worked with Vodafone, BT and KPMG International, whom he represented on the Global Corporate Citizenship Committee of the World Economic Forum. He worked for fifteen years as Chairman of Crime Concern and for nine years on the Commission for Racial Equality. He has been listed as one of the 100 most influential black people in the country. In addition to a

CBE in 2002, he was awarded in 2005 the honour of an independent peerage by the Queen, taking the title '*Baron Hastings of Scarisbrick,* of Scarisbrick in the county of Lancashire.' In the same year – 2005 – he received the UNICEF Award for his 'outstanding contribution to understanding and effecting solutions for Africa's children.' He is president of a development aid agency focused on Zimbabwe. As if to make up for his self-confessed mediocrity at GCE Advanced Level, he was awarded an honorary doctorate in civil law from the University of Kent, Canterbury, in recognition of his leadership at KPMG and the BBC in work for International Development and Corporate Responsibility.

Reflecting on his school days some years after leaving, Michael wrote about 'Four very happy years – immensely rich in opportunity and a superb foundation for later life. Scarisbrick Hall was more an experience of positive enhancement than just a school. It was a school too – good standards and good teachers. They took their lead from Mr Oxley. Studious and sturdy – strong and sensitive.'

In 1975, Michael Hastings was the Sixth Form student whom Charles Oxley appointed to lead twenty-three senior boarders at Scarisbrick Hall in monitoring a full week's television programmes; they were to take detailed note of all instances of swearing, blasphemy and vulgarity before 9.30 p.m. each evening, as well as making judgements on individual programmes. They would present their notes for group discussion and write a report on their findings. The group came from a variety of ethnic, religious and cultural backgrounds, so nobody could accuse them of following the lead of their headmaster. The focus was on the two most watched channels of the day, BBC1 and ITV, from the early evening news until closedown.

A Sunday evening play was awarded the title of 'worst programme of the week': fifteen blasphemies and forty-three swear words in an hour, and a play that 'lacked real dramatic quality and relied heavily on offensive dialogue for any semblance of realism.' Sports coverage was commended, but news programmes concentrated too much on wars, strikes, crimes and protests. Commercial advertising brought a mixture of irritation and amusement, but it was noted that advertisements for alcoholic drinks numbered fourteen in just over six hours on Saturday evening. The team spotted the indirect advertising involved in having so many characters in hotels or homes permanently resorting to cigarettes or alcohol.

Charles Oxley made sure that *The Hastings Report* was sent to the press and media at large. Michael Hastings was interviewed on radio and television as well as by newspapers. A huge postbag arrived at Scarisbrick Hall from all over the country. One ninety-year-old lady from Stevenage wrote, 'Scarisbrick boys will be the Hope and Salvation of England!' She would surely have included the Scarisbrick girls if she had known it was a mixed school.

Mr Oxley's address at the 1975 Speech Day included these words: 'I hope Scarisbrick boys and girls will acquire the courage to stand up and speak out against all that is wrong, regardless of criticism or ridicule. The great reformers of the past were men and women with axes to grind, and they kept on grinding them until the sparks flew. From Amos to John the Baptist and Mary Whitehouse.'

It was exactly forty years later that Baron Hastings of Scarisbrick was the guest speaker at the Scarisbrick Hall School Awards Day. His son drove him up from London (and straight back afterwards) to enable him to say to the assembled school, parents and guests that if we are willing to live for God and for others, not for ourselves, then we will become the people we were designed to be, and fulfil the purpose for which we were created.

Pass mark abolished
The government-sponsored Schools Council had almost certainly put pressure on the Examination Boards to change the grading system for GCE Ordinary Level exams. It was decided that there would no longer be a distinction between a 'pass' and a 'fail', but certificates would be issued to candidates awarded grades D, E and F as well as the (former) pass grades A, B and C. Charles Oxley would have none of it. When schools sent their 'O' Level results to the press in August, he stressed that his schools included only those graded A, B or C in the lists. His stance outraged some state schools, but the uproar brought useful publicity in his attempts to maintain standards in yet another area.

A milestone was reached in 1977, when the school's 'O' Level 'pass' rate climbed above six subjects per pupil for the first time. The precise average was 6.407 from two classes and a total of fifty-nine candidates; Mr Oxley pointed out a comparison with Tower College, whose candidates averaged 6.409 – but from only one class.

The school held its first careers convention. A science club was formed. A group of Scarisbrick pupils visited Paris for a weekend and Mr and Mrs Oxley received a letter from the French capital warmly congratulating the school for having such well-behaved boys and girls. SHOSA, the old students' association, was now producing its own magazine, *White Gates*, named in honour of the portals that still grace the front aspect of the Hall, where the drive comes close to the lake.

Headmaster inducted

Another milestone came with the appointment of the present writer as Headmaster. Mr Oxley's life was now so full and busy that he accepted the need to delegate some of his responsibilities elsewhere. He would continue as Principal of both Tower College and Scarisbrick Hall. He and his wife retained overall control of the business side of things, including the buildings, equipment and grounds, and gave me the responsibility for the day-to-day running of the school, including admissions, dealing with parents and jointly with the Principal deciding on the appointment of new staff members.

When Charles Oxley first mentioned the headship to me, I felt I might benefit from a course in educational management, but when I suggested that to him he said, 'I don't want a manager; I want a leader.' I also asked him to respect the fact that my style of leadership might be a little different from his. I was fully committed to the values and aims of the school and would do all that I could to promote the Christian ethos and high academic standards, but I would not, for example, follow his example in having a small pair of scissors in my top pocket to trim the hair of any boy who went beyond the boundaries of acceptability.

My deputy in 1977–78 was Geoffrey Charrett, succeeded the following year by John Sutton-Smith when Geoffrey left to return to a mixture of teaching and parish work as an Anglican minister.

In addition to the two schools, Charles Oxley made regular trips to India – ten in total – to assist Christian men in that country to set up and run an orphanage, a Bible College and other institutions. He was also a regular speaker in Brethren churches and conferences, in addition to his involvement in crusades, campaigns and committees. He hated to be idle. He had always played his part in the upbringing of his children, but as they grew up, time previously spent with them could be allocated to other things. If he could have survived without meals and sleep, he would probably have done so, as they imposed limitations on the amount of time he could put to other uses.

In 1978, Michael Foot MP, who was Employment Secretary and would soon become Leader of the Labour Party, introduced the May Day bank holiday in Britain; he wanted to show solidarity with workers behind the Iron Curtain who celebrated 1st May as International Workers' Day. Mr Oxley strongly disapproved of what he called 'a Communist Bank Holiday.' Unfortunately, I was unaware of his strong opposition and assumed that everyone was obliged to implement the Government's decision. I had therefore sent a letter to parents and guardians about arrangements for the Bank Holiday Monday, but when the Principal found out what the Headmaster had done, it would be a massive understatement to say that Mr Oxley was not happy. As it happened, the first May Day holiday was a total washout weatherwise, but Scarisbrick Hall School never observed it again while the Oxleys were in charge.

Maximum numbers
1978–79 saw pupil numbers top 700 for the first and only time in the Oxley era, with 130 in the Kindergarten, 148 in the Junior School and 423 in the Senior School. Numbers of girls (45%) had now almost caught up with boys (55%). In the North-West ISA Athletics Championships the Scarisbrick boys were overall winners for the sixth year in succession, while the girls were, as usual, beaten into second place by the Loreto Convent School from Greater Manchester.

Numbers of boarders, however, were now in steady decline from the high point of 130. Local authorities no longer had money to release for expatriate families to have their children at boarding school in the UK, and the fees themselves were rising year by year. Even with discounts, the missionaries and other Christian workers were less likely to be able to afford boarding fees, although Scarisbrick Hall always kept fees at the low end of the independent school range.

Demand for places for four- to six-year-olds remained high, necessitating a rebuild of a whole section of the original stables in the courtyard for a Kindergarten block of six classrooms. The main Hall building was now used mainly for administration and boarding accommodation, with teaching mostly in purpose-built classroom blocks and the science block at the rear of the Hall. Art and music occupied courtyard rooms, and the former engine room housed pottery.

Ten Years On

Teaching staff 1965

Scarisbrick Hall
Ormskirk, Lancs.

As from **September 1970,** girls of 8, 9 and 10 years will be admitted to the Lower School, and girls of 11 years will be admitted to the Middle School. The Middle School will be fully co-educational by 1975. The girls will follow the same academic course as the boys.

Girls who have obtained not less than four subject passes at G.C.E. Ordinary level or C.S.E. Grade 1 level will be admitted to the Sixth Form for G.C.E. Advanced level preparation.

For the present girls are being admitted as day pupils and not as boarders.

Notification that girls will be admitted

Ten Years On

Part of the earliest whole-school photograph (1968) shows Mr and Mrs Oxley – furthest right – and David Raynor – furthest left – who became Headmaster in 1977

CHAPTER 5
INTO THE EIGHTIES

Large numbers of children were still being entered for the Senior School Entrance Examination at 11, but the standard overall in 1979–80 was not good. Pupils coming up from Scarisbrick Hall's own Junior department took the same entrance exams as external candidates, but they did have an advantage both in the way they were taught and in having some idea of what to expect in the exam. Past papers were never issued to either internal or external candidates, as a matter of policy, but a child who had been taught from the age of four or seven at Scarisbrick would have a good chance not only of passing the entrance exam but also of succeeding in the Senior School course.

Again, it was a matter of policy not to lower the pass mark in years when the overall standard was mediocre, even if that meant having a two-form intake at eleven rather than what had become the normal three-form intake.

At the other end of the school, GCE Advanced Level results continued to improve. 1980 was not the first year in which candidates achieved an average over two subjects each, but the grades were encouraging, with more than 50% awarded A or B.

Walking in Wales
From the very beginning, Scarisbrick Hall School pupils happily raised money for charities. Initially, that was always

War on Want, but after a few years it was agreed that other charities should be supported. In 1980 the Bible Society were commemorating the walk undertaken by Mary Jones, a young Welsh lass, 100 years earlier, when she heard that she could get hold of a Bible in the Welsh language. The twenty-six-mile walk took her from her tiny hamlet of Llanfihangel-y-pennant, south-west of Tal-y-Llyn lake, up to Bala, and she was rewarded for her efforts by being given one of the first Welsh Bibles.

Mr and Mrs Oxley decided to throw it open to all pupils and staff at the two schools, Tower College and Scarisbrick Hall, to devote a school day to replicating Mary Jones' walk and to raise as much sponsorship money as possible for the Bible Society. One hundred and ten Scarisbrick pupils took up the challenge, plus a handful of staff, including the headmaster and the head of the Junior School. Mr and Mrs Oxley saw to the hiring of coaches and the provision of packed lunches for the troops, and they took a full part also in the event itself. Mrs Oxley did the walk and because all but the first 200 yards was on tarmac, she did not bother with stout walking shoes or boots. She set off very early, well ahead of the school parties, who in fact saw her coming towards them as the coaches headed south to the starting-point, several miles further on. Her stride was never long, but her courage and determination were huge, and she duly completed the course without any fuss.

Her husband's role was as marshal and chief intermediary between the massed ranks and the local constabulary and pub landlord. The latter was not thrilled when dozens of youngsters took a breather and a lunch break in his pub car park, although there was neither trouble nor litter. The police took some persuading that busy roads without pavements were suitable for this small army to be walking along. Whether or not Mr Oxley contacted the police before the event, his shuttling up and down the stretched-out phalanx of bodies and called-out reminders to walk in single file paid dividends, as all finished safely in Bala, where a service was held in the church to give thanks for the work of the Bible Society. The total raised from sponsorship exceeded £3,000, equivalent to perhaps £10,000 in 2024.

Another special event took place in 1980 with a visit by a Royal Navy helicopter, which landed on the school playing field. A display team performed before the assembled school and the Senior School were given an understanding of the United Kingdom's role in NATO.

Enter Rachel Oxley
In 1980–81 both the Kindergarten and Juniors had two classes per year for the first time. Among the additional staff needed to cope with this influx came Miss Rachel Oxley, former pupil and future Head of Kindergarten before becoming Principal. This was to be her most enjoyable period of involvement with Scarisbrick Hall School. At Tower College she had been one of several of the Oxley clan, whereas at Scarisbrick she and brother Michael stood out more and, perhaps unsurprisingly, did not feel at home in the way that they did at The Towers. Then, in her later incarnation as Principal, after the death of both her parents, the full weight of responsibility for the school and its financial viability rested on her shoulders. But, when she joined the Kindergarten staff, trained and ready to teach a class of twenty or so eager and responsive six-year-olds, she was absolutely in her element.

In the early 1980s Mr Oxley hit the newspaper headlines. Liverpool Bible College, of which he was Principal, was housed in premises in the Toxteth area of Liverpool. When the Toxteth riots took place, the College building was right at the heart of the area under attack. He stayed through the night of unrest, with a fire extinguisher in every room. The rioters had wanted to take over the building as their headquarters, but Charles Oxley defied them.

Amazingly – and surely, only by the protection of God – the college remained untouched, with not even a single window broken, while a nearby cinema, a century-old Racquets Club and a bank were either burnt out or reduced to rubble. Liverpool Bible College would later occupy rooms in the main building at Scarisbrick Hall.

Meanwhile, educational standards at Scarisbrick Hall continued to rise. Fifth Formers were now achieving an 80% 'pass' rate (Grades A – C) at 'O' Level and an average of seven subjects each. The Upper Sixth were averaging three A-level passes each and a pass rate of about 70%.

More than 70 pupils were now having individual instrumental music lessons at school; they also played in smaller ensemble groups and the concert band, all of which featured in musical evenings, both in school and in the Floral Hall, Southport.

In 1982–83, the number of girl pupils finally caught up to equality with the boys. Exam results that year were outstanding: an 80% 'pass' rate at 'O' Level and 83% of candidates passed in five or more subjects, against a national average of 22%. At A-level, the pass rate was 88%, with an impressive average of 3.6 subject passes per candidate.

School Number Three
Meanwhile, 'Christian Schools North-West Ltd.' became 'Christian Schools Ltd.' when Hamilton College became part of the company alongside Tower College and Scarisbrick Hall

Into the Eighties

School. Charles Oxley had received approaches from various individuals and groups over the years about taking over failing schools, but this was different. Here he was, in his early sixties, running two flourishing schools, a Bible college and a lot of moral campaigns, and suddenly he takes the necessary steps to start a third school 205 miles north of Tower College. Why?

Part of the answer lies in Charles Oxley's childhood. The divorce of his parents, at a time when his father was a respected member of the Christian Brethren movement, caused such a shock in the Brethren assembly where the family worshipped that Charles' mother took the four children away from St Helens to go and live in Glasgow. She was born in Hamilton. Divorce was much less common in those days than it is today, particularly among Christian couples, and the sense of shame was strong. The children became labelled as the 'poor Oxley bairns'; so when, fifty years later, Charles had the opportunity to set up a new school in his mother's home town, the project really gripped him as a way of showing that this 'Oxley bairn' had been able to overcome any obstacle caused by his parents' divorce.

It was Muriel who sowed the seed in Charles' mind. She had attended a baptismal service in Hamilton, held in the heated indoor swimming pool of the College of Education, which was about to close down. The four-storey building, erected in the 1960s for £2 million, with fifty-one acres of grounds including playing fields, contained a 1,000-seater auditorium, lecture rooms, science laboratories, art and music rooms, two gyms, a large sports hall and the swimming pool. When the Oxleys' sealed bid of £270,000 was found to have been successful, the local Labour MP, George Robertson, and the Labour-controlled council protested loud and long. The sale and its repercussions even reached the Public Accounts Committee of the House of

Commons. How could a valuable publicly-owned facility be sold off so cheaply to a private educational entrepreneur?

Hamilton College opened as an independent school on 27th August 1983 with 287 pupils. Charles Oxley's weekly commute now looked like this:

> Early Monday morning: drive 205 miles from home at Tower College to Hamilton College and spend the rest of Monday there and all day on Tuesday.
>
> Tuesday evening: return to Tower College. Wednesday: divide the day between Tower College and Scarisbrick Hall School.
>
> Thursday: early morning drive up to Hamilton for the rest of that day and all of Friday. In the early days of the new venture spend Saturday morning at Hamilton for prospective parents' show-rounds, etc. Return to Tower late Saturday night.

Hamilton College had the same clear Christian ethos as Tower and Scarisbrick. Considerable numbers of ethnic Asian families came flocking to the new school. Although they were nearly always Muslims, they were happy for their children to learn about the Christian faith. What they wanted was high academic standards and high standards of behaviour. They particularly valued propriety towards girls, which some of these families found was lacking in state schools.

One consequence of the opening of Hamilton College was the loss of two teachers from Scarisbrick Hall. Lockhart McEwan and Fiona Boyle had both been resident staff, teaching in Kindergarten and Juniors respectively, and adding much to the Christian ethos of the school. Both came from the Hamilton area and were thrilled at the opportunity to teach in a Christian school 'back home.' Their departure was felt particularly keenly on the boarding side at Scarisbrick, as it was becoming increasingly difficult to find good quality resident staff who would commit themselves not only to the classroom but also to the boarding pupils in the evenings and at weekends.

Labour politicians continued to rail against the Hamilton school and its Principal and proprietor. In a Commons debate in 1986 on Scottish Tertiary Education, George Foulkes MP spoke of

> *... the scandal of the sale of the Hamilton College buildings at a knockdown price. They were sold to a somewhat dubious character who is also involved in a pretty sinister campaign for law and order. To sell Hamilton College to a sort of Mary Whitehouse in trousers is not a sensible step. I hope that the Minister will get his inspectors to look at what is going on in that private institution. It would bear very careful scrutiny.*

A little more scrutiny on Mr Foulkes' part would have prevented him from making himself look rather silly. Two weeks before he made these remarks, eighteen members of Her Majesty's Inspectorate of Schools had completed a six-week investigation of Hamilton College, as a result of which the Scottish Education Department granted the school full registration. Charles Oxley wrote to ask him to withdraw his offensive remarks, but he refused to do so.

Second foreign language
The Scarisbrick Hall curriculum now had German as a second modern foreign language alongside French, and pupil

exchanges were organised, with German pupils spending time at Scarisbrick before roles were reversed and Scarisbrick pupils went to stay with the German families. Ski holidays were well established: the party heading to Austria in 1984 was the sixteenth consecutive annual trip. At Speech Day that year the guest speaker was David Jones, one of the original pupils, who had gone on to be a local councillor and was also the chairman of the Scarisbrick Hall Old Students Association (SHOSA). When girls became part of the school population, the Old Boys' Association had a choice to make: should it evolve into the Scarisbrick Hall Old Boys' and Girls' Association? It was decided that a more acceptable acronym than SHOBAGs would be SHOSA. Later generations seem to have decided that 'alumni', with its Latin – and therefore superior-sounding? – origin, should replace 'old boys' and 'old girls.'

The Scarisbrick uniform of maroon blazer and pale blue shirt or blouse was required through to the Fifth Form (Year 11). In the Sixth Form, the boys wore a black blazer, but the only variation for Sixth Form girls had been to have a grey skirt instead of a maroon one; the blazer was still maroon. It was agreed in 1984–85 that the Sixth Form girls should wear a grey business-style suit, marking them out as being well on the way to 'the big wide world' beyond school.

Little ones
The length of the school day was also adjusted. By reorganising the lunch sittings, the lunchtime break was reduced by fifteen minutes, enabling afternoon lessons to finish at 4.00 instead of 4.15 p.m.. Even so, the length of the working day was still greater at Scarisbrick Hall than at most schools and could be regarded as a trade-off for the longer holidays that Scarisbrick pupils enjoyed.

Into the Eighties

The Kindergarten (KG) had now been in operation for ten years. A team of dedicated teachers had been led throughout that decade by Mrs Doreen Lisle, who had now reached retirement. Her place was taken by Rachel Oxley. With their own staff room in their modern suite of rooms in the courtyard, and their daily routine being quite different from Juniors and Seniors, KG teachers lived a largely separate life for much of the time. They, of course, set standards and expectations among the youngest children which would serve them well as they progressed up the school. The bonds between Kindergarten pupils and their teachers were usually long and strong. KG staff looked on with knowing pride as their little darlings grew into accomplished musicians, scholars or sports players. In later years, when one child who had started at Scarisbrick in KG1 was eventually appointed as Head Boy in the Upper Sixth, Miss Oxley and her colleagues remarked, 'We knew from the age of four that he was a future Head Boy.'

The Senior School Entrance Examination now used standardised cognitive abilities tests to try to be as fair as possible to all candidates, irrespective of the Junior School from which they had come. Inevitably, though, there were still borderline cases where it was a matter of perhaps giving a child the benefit of any doubt about his or her ability. As long as parents realised that admission in these circumstances was on a trial basis, there was every reason to hope that good teaching and the right attitude on the pupil's part would bring about success. One such pupil was admitted as a borderline at 11, but went on to gain six subject passes at GCE Ordinary Level, four subject passes at Advanced Level in 1985, an Honours degree in Modern History and Politics at the University of Liverpool and a commission at the Royal Military Academy, Sandhurst.

An outstanding achievement in a different sphere was that of Angus McNab, very much a local boy, as he lived with his mother and sister just a couple of hundred yards from the main entrance to the Scarisbrick Hall grounds. He always had a strong social conscience allied to his Christian faith, and in the summer of 1985 he cycled from Land's End to John O'Groats, raising over £600 for Save the Children to help the poor and hungry in Africa.

Form teachers encouraged their classes to try and think of creative ways of raising money for charity, but all too often they would fall back on the well-tried method of having a lunch-time tuck shop. As Headmaster, I recall actually banning tuck shops during one term to try and force a more original approach which did not involve the self-indulgence of eating cakes. On another occasion I challenged them in the style of the Parable of the Talents by giving each class a ten-pound note and encouraging them to use their ingenuity to multiply it as much as possible. A new hospice – Queenscourt – was being built in Southport, and Scarisbrick pupils contributed £1523 to the appeal.

CHAPTER 6
A Pioneer Passes On

End of boarding

The year 1985–86 marked the end of boarding at Scarisbrick Hall School. Declining numbers and the difficulties of employing suitable resident staff were major factors. Overall numbers of pupils were down to 530, with girls now outnumbering boys by just ten. Half of the teachers had now been at the school at least ten years. Among those who departed that year were Jean Leslie, the School Matron, after thirteen years (she left to be married), and Beryl Yates, who, in addition to her excellent work as a Physics teacher and originator of the Science Club, was an accomplished artist. Among a series of her landscapes in the Lancashire countryside was a striking painting of Scarisbrick Hall in the snow. One of her paintings of the Hall is now displayed in the entrance hall of the school.

The high GCE standards to which Charles and Muriel Oxley had aspired when the school opened in 1964 were now regularly being achieved. In 1985–86 A-level candidates achieved an average of 3.25 subject passes with an 86.7% pass rate. At 'O' Level the Fifth Formers (Year 11) averaged 6.88 subject 'passes' each, with a 78.6% pass rate. But alas, the end had come for 'O' Levels, as the Conservative government decided to replace the two separate exam courses – 'O' Level and CSE (Certificate for Secondary Education) – with one exam, the General Certificate of Secondary Education. One grading system would cover all pupils and schools would need to choose whether to enter pupils for higher grades or lower ones. The phrase 'dumbing down' had not been coined then, but 'fudge' certainly had, and many of the independent schools' associations in particular felt this was a retrograde step in the drive to raise standards.

Alternative renderings for GCSE were suggested:

Government Claims Seem Excessive
Great Conspiracy to Stifle Exams
General Confusion in State Education.

Illness strikes
Now into his sixties, Charles Oxley maintained a brisk pace in his life as he continued to keep so many saucers spinning. He had enjoyed good health throughout his life, but in August 1986 a visit to his doctor brought a sudden and severe shock: he had cancer of the prostate gland, and the disease had also spread to the pelvic bones and lower spine. The only family members to know initially were Muriel and Rachel; Marcus, Michael and Danny would be told later.

Although he stayed out of the public gaze as much as possible, it was evident when he appeared at Sports Days at Tower and Scarisbrick in the summer of 1987 that all was not well with him. His impressive six-feet four-inch stature looked diminished and his cheeks were hollow. His spirit and determination were never in question, but he lacked the energy to do all that he wanted to do. He did manage to scale the mountain of being on the platform for a final Speech Day at each of his three schools.

On 23rd October 1987 he sent out a letter to all parents and members of staff at Tower College, Scarisbrick Hall School and

A Pioneer Passes On

Hamilton College, informing them of his state of health. By then he had relinquished his position as Principal of Hamilton College, although he, Muriel and Rachel would continue on the Board of Governors, of which he retained chairmanship. The school had over 600 pupils and was well established both financially and educationally. The letter concluded:

> *I am able to deal with correspondence and administrative matters and will continue to do so for as long as possible. My wife who started the schools with me – Tower College forty years ago and Scarisbrick Hall twenty-four years ago – has responded marvellously to this new situation. When I am no longer able to discharge my responsibility to the schools, my wife, in addition to her present very heavy commitment to the schools, will assume full responsibility. I am confident that the parents, the teaching and the non-teaching staff will give her full support.*
>
> *I am very thankful for having had 64 years of perfect health and I face the future calmly with a firm faith in my Lord and Saviour, Jesus Christ.*

A little over two weeks later, Mrs Oxley rang me at Scarisbrick to request my presence at Tower, as her husband had things to say to me. He wanted to give me instructions about his funeral and memorial service, as the latter would be my responsibility. Everything was typed out neatly on two A4 sheets, which he handed to me when I was taken into his bedroom by his wife. One week later, she rang me early in the morning to let me know that Charles Oxley had died peacefully the night before.

One School & Two Families

Peter Gregory, one of the first Scarisbrick Hall pupils, had joined the police when he left school, and it was fitting that he should be on traffic control duty outside St Ann's Church in Rainhill when the burial took place, following the service in the Deaf and Dumb Institute in St Helens. Both schools were closed for the day to allow staff and pupils to attend if they wished.

Memorial
A few weeks later, the staff, pupils and parents from both schools took part in a memorial service at the Floral Hall on the Promenade in Southport, the venue for many speech days and musical concerts. As required by the A4 instruction sheets, the hymns were sung 'with gusto ... nothing morbid' and a clear gospel message was brought by the Scarisbrick Deputy Head, John Sutton-Smith. Charles Oxley wanted his death to be a means of offering eternal life to others, and it is known that four people became Christians following the memorial service. Muriel Oxley set the tone, as she had done at the funeral, by standing, dry-eyed, and singing the hymns lustily: 'Lift up your hearts! We lift them, Lord, to Thee', 'We rest on Thee, our Shield and our Defender', and that great affirmation of the resurrection: 'Thine be the glory, Risen Conquering Son.' When asked how she could maintain such equilibrium, she replied, 'I don't grieve for my husband, because he has gone to be with the Lord, which is far better. Grief and tears would be rather selfish, expressing our sense of loss, when really what we want to emphasise is gratitude for his life and achievements.'

Obituaries reflected the controversial and the compassionate in this rare champion of Christian values. Mary Whitehouse, quoted in the *Liverpool Echo,* said, 'I am deeply grieved at his death because he was a man of such immense courage. He showed a simple, uncomplicated commitment to the things he believed to be right and true.' The leader column in that paper said, 'Every parent owes a debt to Charles Oxley, the Merseyside law and order campaigner ... Mr Oxley was uncompromising in his views, some of which were considered extreme even by those who agreed with him on other matters. But he did more than most of us to expose evil and to cause us to think about the way in which society is moving.'

Many knew him only for what he opposed: sex shops, paedophilia, vulgarity and blasphemy in the media, the erosion of Biblical content from Religious Studies courses, over-tolerant church leaders. A few knew him to be a compassionate man who, for example, worked quietly to help and care for victims of domestic violence, as well as contributing significantly to the well-being of the poor in India. His legacy can also be measured in the thousands of young lives whom he influenced for good through setting up three independent schools in which high academic standards, high standards of behaviour and the clear presentation of the Christian faith were absolutely paramount.

New Challenge
Muriel and Rachel Oxley now had big decisions to make. Should they continue their direct involvement in the three schools or commit themselves just to the two English ones? Or would Tower College alone – their home as well as their first school – be a sufficient challenge? Security would be a consideration. There had been occasional vandalism on the premises of Tower College while Charles was still about. And there was a famous occasion when a burglar broke into The Towers (as the main, original building was called) one night

when both Charles and youngest son Danny were at home. It should be pointed out that both father and son were six feet four inches tall and each weighed about sixteen stone. It was after midnight, but Charles was still at work in his study when he heard sounds. Danny had caught the man hiding in the bathroom, and when the man took a swing at him, he received a punch on the head for his trouble. One might almost have had some sympathy for the cornered intruder, pinned down by one Oxley while the other went to telephone the police, had it not been that the miscreant tried to claim that the two men had picked on him and beaten him up!

Muriel Oxley had effectively combined the roles of bursar and domestic bursar for Tower College (forty years), Scarisbrick Hall School (twenty-four years) and Hamilton College (five years). The business and financial side of the company would still be her primary concern, but with Rachel at Scarisbrick, herself at Tower and Hamilton passing into a separate ownership, she felt that the role of Principal was what she had to take on.

With the closure of the boarding side, total numbers declined at the upper end of the school, although the opening of a Nursery in 1989–90 – thanks to the initiative of Rachel Oxley – did improve numbers at the younger end. The departure of the boarders also affected Sixth Form numbers, as the attractions of Sixth Form Colleges drew more and more Year 11 pupils away. King George V in Southport had been the boys' grammar school for the town for generations, but with the comprehensive system now installed, KGV became the local college to go to for A-levels, without uniform and without fees.

Staff changes in 1988 included the departure of Deputy Head John Sutton-Smith (19 years in total), as well as Geoff Roberts, Head of French (22 years), and Marian Snow, Head of

English (16 years). Former headmasters made their mark among the teaching staff. W G Merriman – Bill to many, George to a few – had taught A-level Maths well into his seventies with considerable success and the energy of a twenty-year-old. Ken Masters, a prominent Roman Catholic layman, had been Head of both a public school and a Kirkby comprehensive before 'getting back to real teaching' for his final working years at Scarisbrick. Not only did he teach English superbly to GCSE and A-level, but he set an example to all his colleagues by his willingness to help in so many ways: volunteering to umpire cricket matches, taking morning assemblies – usually off the cuff, it cannot be denied – producing Shakespeare plays with his Sixth Formers and, later on, taking roles in school musicals. His 'old school' approach was typified by his insistence on having a necessary hip replacement on the first day of the summer holidays, so that he could recuperate in time to be back on duty at the start of the new school year in September.

John Sutton-Smith's departure to become a full-time church leader in Southport left a gap in the spiritual leadership in the school. Among many committed Christians who worked at Scarisbrick Hall, he probably did more than any to introduce pupils to the Christian faith and to help many to fulfil the words of the school's motto: 'May you grow in the grace and knowledge of our Lord Jesus Christ.' (The Greek words for 'grace and knowledge' appeared on the school's blazer badge.) John also maintained contact with many of his flock after they left school, and they have always found an open welcome at his home in Scarisbrick and an open heart to offer them counsel.

A new Deputy Head
It might be thought surprising that a school with an evangelical foundation would contemplate having Roman Catholics take

morning assembly, but it was always good to find in one's colleagues that willingness to commit to a weekly slot in the rota. Christian values were the basic requirement, and those who could present truth from the Scriptures had the opportunity to do so. Charles Oxley always said that assembly should be evangelical (i.e. Bible-based) but not evangelistic (applying pressure to secure a response to the gospel message).

The choice of John Sutton-Smith's successor as Deputy Head may also have raised a few eyebrows: Elizabeth (Libby) Wilson had been teaching French and German in the school for five years and was also a Roman Catholic. Despite increasing back pain, she carried out her duties with dignity and compassion. Steve Moran was appointed Senior Master with responsibility for internal and external examinations, and organising Speech Day, but he emigrated to Australia a year later, with Will Chipchase replacing him in the new role.

The school scored well in GCSE examinations, 82% of candidates achieving five subject 'passes' (grades A–C) in 1988. Questions were still being asked about the level of academic rigour in the new examination; for example, with 20% of all candidates nationally achieving an A in French, could it really be true that one in every five sixteen-year-olds across the country was extremely fluent in the language?

National Curriculum
1989 marked the school's twenty-fifth year. Coincidentally, a new, full-size trampoline appeared in the gym; new computers were installed; a promotional video of the school was made. The Conservative government introduced the National Curriculum, setting out standards attainable by every child at every age. As an independent school, Scarisbrick Hall was not required to adhere strictly to the National Curriculum, but

could pick and choose the parts that were beneficial. Not surprisingly, the attainment targets were generally lower than the standards expected of Scarisbrick pupils. It would be necessary to keep abreast of developments, assess, sift, adapt and use anything that enhanced the experience of the pupils.

The implementation of the National Curriculum proved to be a logistical monster for teachers and schools. It was calculated at some point in the process that for every teacher across the country, 1438 sheets of paper had been issued.

The programme for the 1990 Speech Day at Southport's Floral Hall included a full staff list for the first time and the university destinations of Upper Sixth leavers. The guest speaker for the occasion was Peter Dawson, the leader of the Professional Association of Teachers. The PAT took the position of never asking its members to go on strike, whereas the larger unions have always maintained that weapon in their armoury if a government ever failed to come up with an appropriate response to demands on pay and/or conditions of employment.

Mrs Oxley always maintained that Tower College had more of a family feel than Scarisbrick Hall; that was not just down to the fact that the Principal lived on the premises, although that contributed. By now, however, family traditions saw ex-pupils of Scarisbrick sending their children to sit in the same seats in the same rooms as their parents. The 'family feel' was also enhanced by one family – the Haiders – having five children in the school at the same time.

On the non-teaching side, the school benefited from the many years of service from the husband and wife team of Dennis and Brenda Wood, caretaking, cleaning and making themselves generally useful. Dennis in particular had shown great patience with teachers who questioned why the central heating did not stay on through the day in cold weather. He was under orders with a strict timetable to keep heating costs as low as possible, but there were plenty of occasions when science teachers had Bunsen burners lit for purposes other than scientific experiments.

Results at Advanced Level continued to impress, with an 87% pass rate in 1990 and an average of 3.42 subject passes per candidate. One quiet, studious young man stood out even so: Stephen Benge added five A grades at A-level to the nine A grades he had already gained in GCSE two years earlier, thus securing his place at the University of Durham.

The school's fund-raising for charity also hit the heights, £2,000 being sent to India to build an extension to an orphanage which Mr Oxley had set up.

Scarisbrick Hall was still the fifth largest school among the membership of over 300 schools in the Independent Schools Association. Mrs Oxley decided that the school's membership of ISA should now be in the name of the Headmaster rather than the Principal. It was always interesting to attend day conferences on various matters, and I valued the opportunity to share and learn from the experiences of other Heads.

The school's house system originally divided pupils into four groups to compete as teams on Sports Day in the Juniors and Seniors. Now it made an impact more widely and throughout the school year. One element was Progress Card points. Progress Cards were introduced in the early 1970s, showing attainment grades and effort grades for each subject; it was the effort grades which earned house points. Progress Cards were issued about twice a term, to keep parents up to date with how their offspring were doing, to supplement the information given in the end-of-term reports. Inter-House competition also included netball, football, tennis, public speaking and a general knowledge quiz.

A Pioneer Passes On

This quaint building served as a Pottery room and a girls' changing room and is now incorporated into the Oak Theatre complex as a cafe

One School & Two Families

The Hall grounds have various interesting features including this boat house

Scarisbrick Hall

A Pioneer Passes On

Muriel Oxley on a sponsored walk

One School & Two Families

SHOSA members in 1985

A typical Speech Day group (1994):
(l to r) Philip Ashton, Head Boy; Miss Wright, Head of Junior School;
Mr Chipchase, Senior Master; Mrs & Mr Cotterall, Guest Speaker; Mr & Mrs
Raynor; Mrs Draper, Head of Kindergarten; Miss Oxley; Laura Kamel, Head Girl

CHAPTER 7
THE NINETIES

The school still had numbers in excess of 500 pupils aged from three in the Nursery to eighteen in the Upper Sixth. Class sizes averaged fifteen in Nursery and Kindergarten, twenty-two in the Junior and Senior departments. Information Technology (IT) was now widely accepted as a subject in the curriculum of schools, and Scarisbrick was no exception. Increasingly, however, the emphasis shifted, with computers becoming a tool to be used in the classroom for the benefit of a range of subjects, much as overhead projectors had become established. Nevertheless, the time-honoured chalk-and-talk method continued to be the teaching style of many members of staff.

In 1990–91, Scarisbrick Hall School initiated a work experience programme for its Fifth Form (Year 11). The period after the end of GCSE examinations had always been something of a challenge for staff, knowing that in most schools, exam candidates were free to be away from school once the final paper had been completed. While there were still boarders in school, it was expected that all pupils would stay in normal attendance and staff would try to come up with ideas to keep the Fifth Formers interested and occupied. The increasingly effective careers staff suggested and implemented work experience. Many parents and other contacts with their own businesses or professions gladly offered two weeks for Fifth Formers to find out at first hand what a real work environment felt like.

League tables

Along with the National Curriculum and the GCSE came another element of the nationwide educational picture which was not universally popular: league tables. The familiar epithet about 'lies, damned lies and statistics' was dusted off and applied ad nauseam as one group or another claimed that raw numbers did not tell the full story. Averages of GCSE or SATs (Standard Attainment Tests) results were all very well, but they did not initially differentiate between a school in a middle-class suburb and a school in a deprived inner-city area. A formula was devised to include in the calculations 'value added' to try and measure the scale of improvement from secondary school entry at 11 to departure at 16.

The independent sector had its own grounds for complaint, as government GCSE figures related to sixteen-year-olds, whereas many independent schools entered some of their candidates a year early for some subjects. Their results were excluded, thereby giving a false impression of the sixteen-year-old cohort. Again, in the lists which appeared in the national press, schools with small numbers of GCSE or A-level candidates were excluded, the assumption apparently being that with a smaller number of pupils you really ought to achieve better results.

Some of these anomalies were eventually addressed by the *Financial Times*, which, in 1992, produced an index of 500 independent schools. Criteria included the number of pupils in the school, the number in the Sixth Form, the examination results, admissions to higher education institutions (universities, polytechnics and colleges) and, crucially, tuition fees. I write 'crucially' because Scarisbrick Hall under the Oxley regime prided itself on keeping fees within reach of middle-income families prepared to make a sacrifice for the benefit of their children. Only three schools out of the 500 charged lower fees than Scarisbrick Hall. Many schools which charged far more achieved only comparable or inferior results.

It certainly helped to show the school in a good light that its pass rate in 1992 exceeded 92% in both GCSE and A-level; the average number of subject passes per candidate was 8.27 at GCSE and 3.54 at A-level, both being the school's best ever. Despite the fact that someone wrote to *The Times* to suggest that GCSE now stood for Guaranteed Certificate for Sitting the Examination, Scarisbrick Hall deserved the plaudits its Fifth and Upper Sixth Formers were achieving. Miss Oxley now introduced a new-style, glossy prospectus and also started a tradition of Open Days to enable parents to see at first hand just what the school had to offer. She also arranged for the production of a promotional video of the life of the school.

In 1993, the school's A-level pass rate reached 94%, which made it all the more disappointing that the school was still battling to persuade Fifth Form pupils that their prospects were excellent if they stayed on in the Sixth Form. The *Financial Times* again put things into a national perspective with their correlation between results and fees. Scarisbrick Hall's results placed them third in the whole country and best in the North of England. In the years that followed, the school was placed in the top six every year in the FT survey.

Individuals
Sometimes it is events out of school that make one stop and think, as, for example, when a pupil is killed in a car accident, as happened twice within a few years. Another sad death – this

time a former pupil – made news in all the media in 1992. Julie Stuttard, as she was before she was married, went over to South Africa for a holiday with a friend she had known from college days. They were both sunbathing on a beach when they were brutally murdered. Julie had worked as a marketing director, but she also devoted time to teaching inmates at a young offenders' institution in Leicester. Another former pupil who risked his life more than once was James Mawdsley, a campaigner for democracy in Burma who was twice imprisoned under the notorious military regime for his illicit activities trying to help alienated tribes in that country.

Happier stories were written about Adam Thornton, a seventeen-year-old pupil, who was a passenger in a light aircraft when it crashed on Scafell during a storm in the Lake District. Dazed but uninjured, he had the presence of mind to look for help before going back to the plane to look after the pilot tutor and a trainee flier, staying with them for thirty hours until the emergency services arrived. When he eventually reached home, he had just five and a half hours sleep before having a check-up with his doctor, then returning to the Woodvale aerodrome, where he was a member of the aero club. With the chief instructor on board, he took the controls of the Piper Cherokee – identical to the one that had crashed – and in the words of the instructor, 'He didn't make one mistake and he made a very good landing. I think this whole episode reflects his courage.'

When Charles and Muriel Oxley bought Scarisbrick Hall in 1963, they made an agreement with Lancashire County Council that members of the public would be able to visit the Hall on a specified date each year to see the carvings and other artworks. Other groups, such as historical societies, were also able to make arrangements to visit and view. One keen and

The Nineties

knowledgeable member of the Victorian Society was Andrew Lloyd-Webber, who, in the days before he became a noble Lord, was already famous for his musical theatre productions such as *Phantom of the Opera*. When he was invited to switch on the illuminations at Blackpool, he telephoned to see whether he and his then wife, Sarah Brightman, could stop off to have a look at one of the finest examples of neo-Gothic architecture in England, Scarisbrick Hall.

With eyes uplifted and guidebook in hand as he stepped out of the chauffeur-driven limousine, he almost purred with delight at what he saw. He obviously knew far more about the Pugins and their work than I did, so I quickly realised that the patter I used so often when showing prospective parents around was quite unnecessary. As we walked from the Red Drawing Room into the Kings' Room through the huge oak doors, I mentioned that Mr and Mrs Oxley had paid just over £24,000 for the Hall. He paused, reflected for a moment, then said, 'Today, **these doors** would be worth £24,000!'

Musical theatre on a less exalted scale was also about to make an entry among the school's extra-curricular activities. Apart from Sixth Form productions of *Othello* and *Measure for Measure*, the school had been without a school play for about twenty years. During my time as Head of English we had produced George Bernard Shaw's *Arms and the Man*, Sheridan's musical play *The Duenna* and a 'Whitehall farce', *Post Horn Gallop*. Successive English staff, however, had other priorities than drama. When Dr Brian Hodge joined the staff as Head of Music in 1992, among his many attributes he had regularly accompanied local musical societies for their productions. Over lunch one day in the dining hall, it was suggested to him that the school could perhaps put on a musical, such as *Oliver*. He agreed.

Music was now well established in the school, with dozens of pupils of all ages having individual instrumental lessons and a concert band of up to ninety. The school certainly had some good singers, although one might not have guessed that from the level of participation in singing a hymn at morning assembly. Although Brian Hodge had agreed to be musical director, it came as a shock after the casting had been done and rehearsals were in full swing when he moved on at Christmas 1993, with the show scheduled for the end of the Spring Term. More than 100 pupils, staff and parents were already involved in performing, set design and construction, set decoration, choreography, make-up, costumes, backstage hands and front of house personnel. It would have been a great pity to lose the momentum and teamwork which had already been generated by the project. It was a considerable relief to be able to appoint Helen Davies as Head of Music, as she had experience as a percussionist with the English Ballet Company and was keen on musical theatre. She quickly organised and rehearsed a small orchestra, writing the score for each instrument, and the project went ahead as planned.

Death of a dedicated lady
A major milestone for the school came in December 1993 with the sad death of Mrs Muriel Oxley, the Principal of Tower College and Scarisbrick Hall, a few days after suffering a stroke. She had worked tirelessly from the start with a rare mix of self-sacrifice, determination and a serving heart, devoted to her husband and her four children, and fully committed also to the success of the schools. Where Charles might have wanted to apply the educational accelerator, Muriel had sometimes applied the business-wise brake, although she fully shared her husband's aims and hopes. She

had acted as bursar and domestic bursar for both schools. 'Mrs Wife', as her husband usually referred to her, was diligent in dealing with school correspondence and with parents while he was busy with his campaigns. She also looked after all the mundane things such as carpets, wallpaper, toilet rolls, laundry and catering; and she had responsibility for kitchen staff, domestic staff, school vehicles and the provision of equipment – so many vital areas covered so faithfully.

If you stand in the main corridor of the Hall and let your eye move upwards, you will gain some idea of the size of the task of replacing wallpaper, as it stretches to the upper storey. And it could not be just any old wallpaper – it had to replicate the Pugin original, to maintain the high standards understandably required by the County Council, English Heritage and the historical societies. Mrs Oxley's love of pink and pale blue became something of a standing joke in the family, but she was very adept in introducing those colours, for example, to the crockery used on occasions such as Sports Days.

The role of Principal, by her own admission, made fresh demands on her, for she shunned the spotlight. She knew that social attitudes in Scotland did not look favourably on a woman as Principal of Hamilton College, so she was glad to free herself of that responsibility. When ownership of Hamilton passed from Christian Schools Ltd., she chose to hand over the four-storey building without cost to the new owners, because she believed so strongly in the value of maintaining the College's clear Christian foundation and teaching.

Muriel Oxley was never one to make a fuss. When her husband was away overnight, she accepted that she and daughter Rachel would spend the night alone in The Towers. When doctors found a cancer in her body, she arranged to have the surgery done during a half-term holiday so that only the very minimum of people even knew about it and she was back at work four days later, having driven herself home from the hospital.

She was also very methodical. From her work as a photographer, she had dozens of albums, every photograph labelled and referenced. She made lists of everything – cutlery, crockery, desks, chairs, tablecloths, the latter including the exact dimensions of the cloths used on the tables at Speech Day in the Floral Hall. She found fulfilment in doing her duty. I recall leaving my office one evening well after school hours, and there in the Great Hall at the top of a twelve-foot step ladder was Mrs Oxley, adding the decorations to the huge Christmas tree which she provided year after year. The step ladder looked none too safe and the lady at the top of it might have appeared out of place and vulnerable; but she saw it as her duty, so she got on and did the job. The hymns sung at the memorial service on 3rd February 1994 were highly appropriate: *For all the saints who from their labours rest* and *He who would valiant be.*

Rachel Oxley knew at first hand exactly what the job description was as Principal of Tower College and Scarisbrick Hall. Although she has no recollection of it being openly discussed, there had always been an assumption that she would continue the Oxley family's leadership of the schools. She appreciated now having her three older brothers on the board of governors: Marcus and Michael were married with growing families; Danny had experience of teaching music in schools before becoming the organiser of European musical tours to such places as Salzburg, Milan and Vienna. When Rachel took up the reins as Principal, Mrs Pam Draper took over as Head of Kindergarten.

Thirty Years On

Scarisbrick Hall School was now thirty years old and, as if to celebrate the anniversary, the Fifth and Upper Sixth both produced the school's best ever examination results. A-level candidates had a 100% pass rate, averaging 4.13 subject passes each. League tables now worked on a points system, with ten points for an A, eight for a B, six for a C, and so on. On that basis, Scarisbrick had the best results of any independent school in Lancashire and Merseyside, as well as ranking 40th in the whole country. GCSE candidates achieved an average of 8.13 subjects (Grades A – C) and a 100% success in gaining five or more subjects.

Anyone who paints a ceiling or weeds a garden can immediately see the results and feel a sense of satisfaction as your efforts are rewarded. To educate a child is quite different. Certainly, there are moments of triumph and transformation along the way, but the wise teacher will withhold judgement as to a child's 'success.' Life throws experiences at us, some of them so unexpected or tough that we cannot be sure whether we have the resources to cope. Scarisbrick Hall pupils were not immune, for example, to the growing trend of parents divorcing. What we do notice and value are the positive ways in which a youngster deals with life's hurdles, because they are rare indeed who seem to have everything handed to them on a golden platter. A distinction in a music exam or a winner's medal in sport is usually the result of many hours of dedicated hard work. And some of the most important things in life may never receive an award at all: thoughtfulness, perseverance, generosity, modesty, integrity. These are the kinds of values that all schools aim to inculcate in their pupils, and to see them exemplified in a young person of any age is a pure delight.

The Christian foundation and teaching at Scarisbrick Hall in the days of the Oxley family led to pleasing numbers of former pupils taking up strategic roles in churches and Christian organisations. In the Headmaster's report to Speech Day in 1994, mention was made of some of these: an associate pastor in Devon, a missionary teacher in the Seychelles for over ten years, the pastor of a Baptist church in Hertfordshire, a pastor's wife in Hull, a church leader in Appley Bridge, a commissioned officer in the Church Army, an evangelist/pastor in Hampshire and a curate in Middlesex. Again, however, it is not just the prominent ones that matter: every person having a quiet influence for good is to be applauded, whatever the sphere of involvement.

Visitors to an Open Day in November 1994 would have seen a computer room twice the size that it used to be: bedroom walls in what had been the 'New Wing' in 1964 were now removed to provide bigger rooms and additional teaching space. The Kindergarten and Nursery had now expanded to take over rooms that boarders would remember as the sick bay. New roofs and ceilings had been built on two of the teaching blocks behind the main Hall. The Sixth Form Common Room had been completely refurbished, and a new Sixth Form Study Room provided individual carels for the students. Rachel Oxley now employed contract cleaners and contract caterers, and she installed closed circuit television cameras. Ironically, soon after the installation of the cameras, they served their purpose in helping to trace a couple of car thieves. David Gray, the boys' P.E. teacher, was taking a group out to the playing field when he commented that a car driving out of the grounds looked very similar to his. He then did a double take when he realised that it was his car being stolen!

Perhaps someone took exception to his role as Fagin in the school's production of *Oliver* and wanted to get their own back! David was by this time contributing significantly to pupils' wellbeing, having responsibility for pastoral care and also leading the voluntary Christian activities in the Senior School, which were really thriving.

Inspection
Pastoral care is always one of the areas that schools inspectors are keen to monitor, and an Independent Schools Inspectorate team descended on Scarisbrick Hall within a year of Rachel Oxley becoming Principal.

One outcome of an inspection is that needs already identified by teachers, caretakers, office staff, caterers or subject heads can be highlighted by inspectors. Such was the case in the Spring Term 1995, when the inspection team concluded that the school did not appear to give high priority to library provision. They had not taken note of the fact that a plan was already in place to upgrade the Senior School library, from a room full of books where one has to stay silent, to a modern resources centre with improved book provision but also computer facilities and a room designed to be enjoyed as well as worked in. Additionally, funding had already been set aside for employing a School Librarian and for improving library provision in the Junior School as well.

Charles Oxley had never felt the need to take a close interest in the content of each subject's curriculum, with the exceptions of Scripture/Religious Education and English. His concern was that youngsters should grow up knowing what the Bible was about. His twin concern was that youngsters should not have to read literature that could be regarded as unwholesome. He had more than one battle with exam boards whose set texts contained what he regarded as unseemly elements, even though the book was widely seen as a classic. (*Cider with Rosie* was a case in point.)

Mr Oxley was willing to trust an experienced teacher with knowing what to teach in their subject area; there was no need for copies of syllabuses to be submitted for the Head's approval. Judith Heaton, who joined the staff in 1974 at the age of twenty-two and would later serve as Head of the Junior School, recalls: 'I had no scheme of work, just notes/plans of what to teach: we were trusted to do our job correctly in a wonderful setting that encouraged teaching and learning.'

Before the inspection team arrived on 27th February 1995, they expected to have all kinds of paperwork in their possession, relating to resources, staffing, management, curriculum, assessment and premises. What the school had increasingly had to accept was that being 'independent' did not mean that they could go on their own sweet way without regard for national norms; some degree of critical review was necessary and healthy if the school was to be recognised as efficient and fairly compared with other educational establishments.

The actual process of this inspection by a team of five over two and a half days involved discussions with teachers, senior management, the Head and the Principal on all kinds of organisational and managerial matters, as well as observation of part or all of eighty-eight lessons. A final oral feedback was followed by the publication of the report, which referred to the school's 'strong ethos based upon its Christian principles. The quality of the work is good, in spite of severe past financial constraints. ... The school is very well led ... but ... would benefit from having a middle management structure...' The report suggested that a faculty structure, with department heads in charge of their own budgeting, would enable the school to coordinate work in line with the National Curriculum.

Costly compliances
The 'severe past financial constraints' mentioned in the report were perhaps an overstatement of the difficulties of maintaining and developing a thriving school in an old building, while keeping fees as low as possible. The reality, however, was becoming stark. The Hall was struggling to cope with the advancing years. Heavy rain, particularly when accompanied by strong winds, would find cracks and crevices that led to buckets being placed in corridors. No quick visit from a builder or plumber would resolve such problems, as they were structural and expensive to repair.

Additionally, government regulations conspired to drain financial resources at an alarming rate. Every window in the main Hall building now had to have a laminating film over the glass, or the glass would have to be replaced. The sewage plant which had served the Hall more than adequately became a problem. If the flushing system was in use all the time, it worked well, but school holidays and the departure of boarders meant that its use was intermittent, resulting in cleaning chemicals slipping into the stream that ran through, and out of, the lake towards farmers' fields. Unless the sewage plant was corrected, Rachel Oxley faced a £20,000 fine every month until it was fixed. Her only way out was to have the sewage system linked to the mains on Southport Road, half a mile distant. Very expensive, and with no visible benefit to the school.

And then there were the bats. In a property like Scarisbrick Hall, it is hardly surprising that bats take up residence. In the

1990s, it was in the engine house, used by the school as a pottery room. Twenty years later, bats would also hold up a major restoration in the main building, where a corridor of dormitory rooms was being transformed into a new library.

Roof repairs are costly. The flat roofs of classroom blocks built in the 1970s had to be repaired or replaced twice in twenty years. The roof of the main Hall was a totally different proposition, because of the special tiling slabs, large, heavy rectangles of something akin to York stone, which could only be replaced by identical ones. In the 1980s, in Charles Oxley's time, the south-west wing of the Hall had been reroofed at huge cost when dry rot was found to be affecting the structure. Lancashire County Council and the Historic Buildings Trust both contributed to the cost of repairs. (What is now the visitors' car park was originally a beautiful lawn, where cricket nets were installed in the summer term. The heavy machinery used in the reroofing ruined the lawn, so a car park now replaced it.)

Despite the crippling overheads, Rachel Oxley oversaw advance and improvement in the school's performance. In 1995, the GCSE average per candidate reached 8.6 subjects, and the A-level average was 3.77 subjects per candidate, with a 94.2% pass rate. The school joined the Independent Schools Careers Organisation (ISCO), enabling every pupil to have psychometric testing. This meant that careers advisers could see where a child's interests, abilities and strengths might lead, and advice could be given more appropriately.

Personal and social education (PSE) was introduced in Years 7, 8, and 9. Extra-curricular courses in fencing, physiotherapy and self-defence became available for older pupils. The Sixth Form were able to go to Fulwood Barracks to do team-building exercises with the Army, plus shooting, archery and the assault course. The annual ski trip was to the French Alps and as well as the exchange visit with a German school, separate trips were made to France and Germany, while a boys' group toured Malta to play football and basketball matches on the island.

The successful production of *Oliver* in 1994 prompted an ambitious plan to put on what was, in effect, a world premiere of *Chitty Chitty Bang Bang.* Not long afterwards, the professionals got in on the act, but Scarisbrick Hall were there first! Helen Davies recorded the dialogue of the film – with permission, of course – to put together a script, and the production and 'special effects' team made use of strobe lighting to give the impression of a flying car and airship in the school gymnasium.

How much independence?
Ten of the fifteen recommendations of the ISI inspection team were implemented. The other five were quietly ignored. For example, 'Revised schemes of work should follow National Curriculum guidelines and the school should adopt National Curriculum terminology in its documentation.' No, thank you. Everyone understood that KG1 was the first class in the Kindergarten, that J4 was the top class of the Junior School, and that 5X and 5Y were the GCSE classes.

The inspectors had commented on there being 'too little consideration of the beliefs and practices of religions other than Christianity. Pupils would benefit from … a broader approach to the subject' (RE). No, thank you. There was a place to consider other religions, in Sixth Form General Studies, but the Christian faith based on the Bible gave more than enough good material to provide a course that was in keeping with the evangelical Christian foundation of the school.

As a member of the Independent Schools Association, I attended a conference on 'Spiritual and moral values in schools' and was interested to note that when a humanist spoke about there being no need for religion as a foundation for values, hardly any of the 120 delegates gave him a clap. Many independent schools at that time still regarded Christianity as the best starting point from which to pass on ethical and moral values to youngsters in this country.

The final recommendation of the inspectors was that 'the use of corporal punishment should be reconsidered in the context of current attitudes and practices nationally.' More than one national newspaper had featured – or perhaps that should be 'named and shamed' – the handful of independent schools that still included corporal punishment in their range of sanctions. It was so rarely used at this stage that Scarisbrick Hall could well have dispensed with it, particularly as the inspectors mentioned the fact that it was not used for girls. Experience showed that girls in the Junior and Senior departments of the school never seemed to engage in the rare forms of misbehaviour that warranted the use of the wooden paddle, although the Head of Kindergarten might apply a smack to the leg of either a boy or a girl where that was thought to be appropriate for very serious misbehaviour.

Inspectors' recommendations regarding a development plan, in-service training, curriculum development, better co-ordination of subjects through Kindergarten, Junior and Senior departments, all had merit and prompted discussion at staff meetings and senior management meetings. The school looked at ways of improving and increasing the use of computers across the curriculum; of catering more effectively for the needs of children with dyslexia; and complying with the law in having registration twice a day.

Potential death trap?
As the country became much more aware of health and safety issues, Scarisbrick Hall School had its own concerns. The main access point into the grounds has always been from the busy A570 Southport–Ormskirk road, opposite the junction with the A5147 road that leads to Halsall, Maghull and Liverpool. At that time, in the 1990s, there was no speed limit on these roads until one had passed the entrance on the way in to Southport. Drivers probably developed a habit of praying every time they emerged from the school drive on to the main road, especially if they were turning right towards Southport. Over the years there had been several near misses and an occasional minor collision. The bend in the road on the Southport side meant that vehicles accelerating out of the speed limit area might only be seen at the moment when a car or coach was emerging from the school drive.

When a visiting school's minibus was involved in a collision, I wrote to Lancashire County Council to point out – not for the first time – the dangers to parents, pupils, staff and visitors. I asked for action to be taken before someone was seriously injured or even killed: a roundabout, traffic lights, warning signs, speed ramps, an extension of the speed limit area? Surely something could be done.

A detailed analysis of the situation came in the letter from the office of the County Surveyor and Bridgemaster. Part of the problem was that the lodge adjoining the entrance to the school grounds was privately owned and the school had no jurisdiction over the boundary wall of that property. Although the height of the wall had previously been lowered to improve the sight line, the growth of trees and shrubs cancelled out that improvement. The extension of the speed limit area to the Ormskirk side of the entrance was a possibility (which later came into force), but other suggested means of traffic calming had ramifications that made them unacceptable. The tone of the letter was sympathetic as well as pragmatic, concluding: 'It may be that an access route via B5242 Hall Road would be safer than via A570.' That would have meant utilising the back drive from the Hall, which heads north-east from the courtyard, passes beyond the mausoleum (now a private house unconnected to the school) and leads to a junction with Hall Lane. In all the years that the school has occupied the Hall, this drive had been allowed to remain full of large, deep potholes by the local residents who did not want to encourage access to the Hall by that route. Finally, that drive has now been completely closed off, allowing no access into or out of the school grounds. This change has, in fact, been beneficial to the school in terms of safeguarding.

In the 1996 public examination results were again outstanding. 91% of our candidates achieved a minimum of five GCSE subjects at Grades A*–C; 61% of our Fifth Formers had ten or more subject passes. At A-level, our pass rate was 95%, with an average of 3.87 subject passes per candidate.

Following the lead of the *Financial Times* a decade earlier, *The Sunday Telegraph* now produced its value-for-money league table, measuring results against fees levels. Scarisbrick Hall School was placed fifth out of 517 independent schools. Of the four schools ahead of us, three were in Jersey and the other one was a military academy. Wry smiles were the order of the day when it was noted that, for example, Cheltenham Ladies' College was placed 277th, Westminster School 320th and Eton College 443rd.

Mrs Libby Wilson's sterling and unstinting work at Scarisbrick ended – sadly accompanied by cruelly continuous back pain – when she left the school in 1996. Her place as

Deputy Head was taken by Will Chipchase, who had proved his worth in many ways, not least in heading up the Geography department, spearheading the careers service in the school, and even designing and building a revolving stage for the production of *The Sound of Music*.

The Junior School now had its own resources room, which was part-library and part practical/messy room, allowing teachers to keep classrooms in pristine condition. The pottery room, which for a time had become the girls' changing room, reverted to its ceramic status. The library improvements, as promised to the inspectors, had taken place, and three laboratories had been refurbished.

Difficult choices
Sadly, for financial reasons, the continuation of the Sixth Form was in serious jeopardy. To employ a teacher to take a class of four or five students for six or seven periods a week is expensive, when that teacher could be teaching classes of twenty-five pupils. Pupil numbers were healthy lower down the school, but not sufficiently large to counterbalance a small Sixth Form. It was particularly poignant when one heard remarks such as those of a mother attending an Open Day who pointed to a Sixth Form girl and said to her daughter, 'And that's what I want *you* to be like when you grow up.'

The state of the Hall, in particular the roof, was now a matter of concern not only for Miss Oxley and her governor brothers, but also for the County Council. Since the death of her mother in 1993, Rachel had received an increasingly intensive flow of enquiries from the Lancashire authority. What action was she taking to preserve the character of the listed building? Could she produce a plan of action to deal with necessary repairs to the structure of the building? If no action was taken to fix the roof, the County Council would be forced to impose a compulsory purchase order on the Hall.

The growth of the school over thirty years meant that most of the daily activities did not take place in the actual Hall, but in the purpose-built blocks to the rear. The main building housed the administrative offices, senior staff room, library, Sixth Form study room and the Junior School morning assembly, held in the Great Hall, but the first floor rooms were no longer used for the school. The Kindergarten and Nursery, music and art departments lived in the courtyard rooms; the Junior and Senior classrooms and the Science laboratories all occupied single-storey blocks behind the Hall.

Nevertheless, the condition of the Hall was a headache. Having spent about £200,000 in two years on bringing the Hall and the site into line with government regulations, the Oxleys were in no position to consider further large-scale spending. Their mother's estate had not yet been settled and they would inevitably have an inheritance tax bill to pay. Until that was all clarified, Rachel could not satisfy the demands of the persistent Council Conservation Officer, who expressed disbelief at the length of time probate was taking, implying that he believed he was being fobbed off. What she did do was to engage the services of a chartered surveyor, Mike Riley, who did an excellent job of acquainting himself fully with the condition and the problems of the Hall. He presented his report at a gathering of all interested parties, including the County Council's Conservation Officer, English Heritage, the National Trust, the Victorian Society, in all about twenty-five to thirty people. After they had all perused the report, Mr Riley gave clear and authoritative answers to every question that was raised. He demonstrated that the Hall's owners had done all that they could in very difficult circumstances. Those present seemed duly impressed. The Conservation Officer spoke afterwards to Miss Oxley: 'What can I say?' 'Just say sorry,' was her reply.

Local newspapers took up the story. The *Liverpool Daily Post* had the headline: 'Historic school hoping to weather the storms' and referred to 'Scarisbrick Hall School's star-studded status' not being a guarantee against a leaking roof. The *Ormskirk Advertiser*'s headline occupied as much space on the page as the story: 'A new roof would make this school look like a million dollars – almost as much as it will cost.' Rachel Oxley was still Principal of Tower College and she knew that work was needed on the roof there as well. When the wind blew, she would lie awake at night wondering whether it was doing further damage to either building.

The company's finances were now causing concern to the accountant and the bank manager. From them came the initial suggestion that the school would need to close the Sixth Form. Miss Oxley was keen to look at other ways of saving money, but the pressure was undeniable. Some of the strain was alleviated by the sale of Halkyn Castle, a property in North Wales that Mr and Mrs Oxley had bought some years before with the intention of establishing accommodation for victimised mothers and children. Authorities frowned on the idea, as also they did on a couple of other possibilities for the use of the castle.

The run of successful musical productions continued with *The Sound of Music*, in which the Von Trapp children's roles were played by pupils ranging from the Kindergarten to Fourth Year Seniors. One of the stars of the show, playing Captain Von Trapp, was Jeff Shaw, then in the Lower Sixth, who could not have imagined that fifteen years later he would be Headmaster of the school. His mother, Joan, was teaching in the Junior School.

End of Sixth Form

By April 1997 it was clear to the governors that the school could not continue to sustain the costs of the Sixth Form, and on their behalf Marcus Oxley, the eldest of the brothers, signed the letter informing parents of the decision. Those already in the Lower Sixth would be able to stay to complete their A-levels, but there would be no new Lower Sixth in September of that year. The letter concluded:

> *We trust that parents will recognise that this has not been an easy decision to take. Our A Level results have given the school a status among the best in the country, but the long term financial security of the school would be in jeopardy if we did not close the sixth form.*

To say that the letter caused a shock would be like saying that Harrod's is a corner shop. Parents and members of staff, other than senior management, had no inkling that the Sixth Form was under threat. Parents wrote to express their dismay. Some were surprised that the signatory of the letter was Marcus Oxley, not realising that he was chairman of governors. They were also angry that the decision came so late in the academic year.

It is probably fair to say that the nature of governance of Tower College and Scarisbrick Hall, under the company name of Christian Schools Ltd., had changed when Mrs Oxley died in 1993. The next generation of the family took on responsibility at that point, but ISI inspections at both schools brought about a realisation that more professional input was needed to make the board of governors an effective set-up. Marcus, as the eldest brother, acted as chairman of the board in the interim, with Michael and Danny also involved.

The Nineties

News of the Sixth Form closure came just before the GCSE examinations were to begin, so that members of the Fifth Form who were expecting to continue in the Sixth Form now had an uncertain future. Some of the available alternatives were already fully booked for September, but it is greatly to the credit of Margaret Davidson and Heather Brake, both science teachers but now with their careers adviser hats on, that places were found for most Fifth Formers (Year 11) in either schools with a Sixth Form or Sixth Form Colleges or Further Education Colleges in the area. A few students had to go on a waiting list until GCSE results were known, but those two ladies worked very hard to give reassurance to those who had expected to stay on at Scarisbrick.

CHAPTER 8
THE BOMBSHELL

Roof repairs

When the 1997–98 school year opened, Miss Oxley informed a meeting of senior management that a survey of the Hall roof showed estimated costs of £406,000 over a period of ten to fifteen years. Although this compared favourably with Lancashire County Council's publicly announced estimate of £1,000,000, it was still prohibitive. A grant of 40% towards the cost would be available from English Heritage, and a further grant might be forthcoming from West Lancashire District Council. Nevertheless, it was evident to those present at the meeting that Christian Schools Ltd. would find it very difficult to commit something in the order of a quarter of a million pounds to the repairs.

It was during that Autumn Term in 1997 that Rachel Oxley was approached by Eric Borowski, the Head of Kingswood School in Southport, to talk about a possible merger between Scarisbrick Hall and Kingswood. His school was owned by Nord Anglia Education, a company with twenty-two schools in Britain and Europe. The suggestion involved closing Kingswood's premises in Birkdale and bringing the two schools together at Scarisbrick. Nord Anglia would commit significant funding to the restoration of the Hall and the enhancement of the school's facilities.

This appeared to be a heaven-sent rescue plan, to which Rachel and her governor brothers gave careful consideration. They could not see a viable alternative that would enable the school to continue. They did not know then that there were other possible interested parties who might have been able to maintain Scarisbrick Hall School with its evangelical Christian emphasis; one man let it be known, after the sale was announced, that he could definitely have done exactly that, but he knew nothing of the parlous state of the finances of the school or of the upcoming merger.

Merger mayhem
Rachel Oxley wrote to parents on 16th March 1998 to inform them of the merger and to state that

> *as from July 23rd 1998, Kingswood College at Scarisbrick Hall will be run and owned by Nord Anglia Education.*

Parents' meetings were arranged for the 18th and 19th March – just two days after the letter went out – to allow parents to have their questions answered by the new owners.

The first of those meetings, on Wednesday evening, generated considerable heat and little light, as some very angry Scarisbrick parents raised strong objections to what was going on and did not appear to be interested in what the Nord Anglia representatives might have to say. As Headmaster of Scarisbrick Hall, I had a seat on the platform of the school gym where the meetings were held. The point came where the Nord Anglia executives looked distinctly uncomfortable, particularly when one irate man demanded to know 'What does Mr Raynor think about this situation?' I replied that I had known nothing of the merger until two weeks earlier, a response which again brought a degree of pandemonium. I hastened to add that I believed Miss Oxley was actually doing me a service by not consulting me about her plans. I had for some months felt that after thirty years in the school, twenty-one of them as Headmaster, it might be time for a change; I had therefore broached the subject of early retirement with Miss Oxley. When I subsequently heard that she had granted it, and when I then heard about the merger, I was sure that the timing was absolutely right, as there would have been no place for me in the new school.

For the second parents' meeting on the Thursday, things had changed noticeably. For a start, Kingswood pupils, in school uniform, were stationed every few yards at either side of the corridors leading to the gym. I offered to the Nord Anglia people to speak at the outset of the gathering to try and bring some order to proceedings, and they agreed. The evening went ahead much more calmly, although feelings of hurt and betrayal were again expressed.

There was no disguising the fact that the two schools, although just a few miles distant from each other, were very different in nature. Where Scarisbrick maintained a robust traditional academic style, Kingswood endeavoured to tailor education to each child's individual needs. Kingswood was widely recognised for its work with children with special needs, particularly those with dyslexia. Eric Borowski addressed head-on the concerns of some Scarisbrick parents who seemed to think that mixing with 'special needs' children might have a damaging effect on their own children's progress: 'Dyslexia is not something you can catch, like measles,' said Eric.

Divided opinions
Parents felt particularly aggrieved that they had been given only two days' notice of these meetings and only four months' notice of the merger. One parent issued a leaflet with the headline 'S O S – Save Our Scarisbrick!' Others were quoted in the local press, reflecting the range of views being expressed. One with a child at Scarisbrick Hall said, 'I am keeping an open mind, but, to be honest, it is too late anyway to get my son in anywhere else even if I wanted to. I am going to see how it goes but, until we know the nature of the beast, it is premature to jump to too many conclusions.' Others were more polarised in their views. 'I am very upset at the buy-out as Kingswood School has a poor academic record,' said one mother. 'If Kingswood were a thriving school with a reputation of high academic success – as Scarisbrick Hall is – then I doubt the merger would have taken place. I do not call an increase of 19 per cent per term a pleasant surprise, which is the increase in the school fees for my two children aged nine and twelve years.' A Kingswood parent declared that the majority of parents at the Birkdale school were in favour of the merger. 'I think it is very good news,' she said. 'I am sick and tired of hearing all the negative points being made about dyslexic and statemented children at Kingswood by some parents at Scarisbrick Hall and I want to redress this. The two schools coming together can only be a success.'

The Independent Schools Information Service provided figures from which parents could make comparisons between the academic standards of the two schools. Over a five-year period, 1992–96, 69% of Kingswood pupils gained five or more GCSE Grades A*–C as against 94% of Scarisbrick pupils. Over the same period, at GCE Advanced Level, Kingswood students passed an average of 2.87 subjects each, scoring 4.02 points per subject and 11.57 points per candidate; the comparable figures for Scarisbrick Hall were 3.02 average subjects, 6.35 points per subject and 19.19 points per candidate.

A colourful flyer to launch 'Kingswood College at Scarisbrick Hall' was headed: 'A Distinguished Past – A Successful Future.' Another A4 sheet showed the transition from the two schools' names to 'Kingswood College', although the logo bore the intertwined letters KS, not KC as might have been expected. Nord Anglia's press release about the merger stated: 'Kingswood College at Scarisbrick Hall will benefit from a substantial investment on the part of Nord Anglia Education Plc which will include refurbishment of classrooms, large scale repairs to the fabric of the Grade I listed Scarisbrick Hall and the development of fully equipped science laboratories, state-of-the-art information technology, sports facilities and library resources. ... We are confident that Kingswood College at Scarisbrick Hall will be immensely successful in fulfilling parents' demand for a first class coeducational school in this area.'

It was unlikely that current pupil numbers at the two schools could simply be added together to gauge class sizes for the following September; had that been the case, it might have been possible for most, if not all, teachers from both schools to be kept on. Inevitably, however, teachers felt under pressure about their future, particularly in departments where Mr Borowski had told Miss Oxley there would be 'overstaffing': Nursery, Kindergarten, and in the Senior School Art, IT, Music, P.E. and Geography. Mr Borowski asked for pen portraits of each teacher's strengths and history before he conducted interviews with each member of the Scarisbrick staff. When a projected list of form teachers was issued for the new classes in the Senior School for September, just six of the seventeen were Scarisbrick staff. And despite assurances given to Miss Oxley, the Kingswood uniform replaced the distinctive maroon of Scarisbrick Hall.

Final fling
Once the initial thunderbolt had struck, the staff did their best to 'keep calm and carry on' with normal school routines. The Junior School football team excelled themselves in reaching the final of the Loveridge Cup, the trophy for competition amongst all Southport junior schools. Cheered on at Southport FC's Haig Avenue ground by a large number of pupils and parents, the team played out a six-goal thriller, drawing 3–3 and sharing the trophy. The ISA athletics produced five national champions, and two girls' couples won the Under 12 and Under 15 Southport Schools tennis trophies.

Sports Days are always something of a lottery, depending as they do on the weather. They also stir memories. It was one of Charles Oxley's delights to referee the inter-house tug of war at the Senior School sports. At the Kindergarten sports, howls of protest would mix with waves of laughter at the sight of respectable gentlemen cheating in the dads' potato-and-spoon race.

The 1998 Sports Days were almost a washout, rain causing the cancellation of the Senior event and forcing the Juniors into the gym for a 'limited edition.' The Kindergarten and Nursery, by contrast, had a glorious sunny day and a wonderful turn-out of parents, grandparents and friends, as if to mark the end of an era.

Thursday 9th July 1998 was the actual end of Scarisbrick Hall School as originally conceived. The school lost its name and its distinctiveness. Thirty-five years after Charles and Muriel Oxley bought the Hall, their daughter Rachel said her goodbyes. She continued successfully in her role as Principal of Tower College, and, as it approached its seventieth year, the school had maintained its high standards, its numbers of pupils and its financial viability.

The Scarisbrick Senior and Junior Schools joined together in the gym for a 'Final Day Thanksgiving Service', with readings and prayers from pupils and staff members, items from the Junior Choir and the Senior Choir and an address from the retiring Headmaster. The hymns each held a particular resonance. 'May the mind of Christ my Saviour live in me from day to day' was regarded by some as 'the school hymn' and was certainly sung on many occasions, including some Speech Days. 'Great is Thy faithfulness' declares the continuing presence of the God who said, 'I will never leave you nor forsake you.' The twentieth-century hymn, 'Lord, for the years' combines praise, thankfulness and prayer; its first verse reads:

> *Lord, for the years Your love has kept and guided,*
> *Urged and inspired us, cheered us on our way.*
> *Sought us and saved us, pardoned and provided:*
> *Lord of the years, we bring our thanks today.*

My final letter to parents included these words:

> The children have adapted in their minds extremely well to the changes that are occurring; the positive approach of so many is to be commended, whether their future is in the new school here or elsewhere. It has not always been easy to carry on as normal this term; teachers have shown great resilience in keeping focused on their work while trying to clarify their own future.

> ... I am sure we will all wish Miss Oxley continued success in her work as Principal of Tower College. The past year has been a difficult and at times painful one for her, and few of us will ever know of the sacrifices she has had to make. She merits our thanks for shouldering the burden of what her parents established.
>
> ... Scarisbrick Hall School has had a beneficial effect on hundreds of lives, but none of it would have happened without the pioneering vision of Charles Oxley and the determination of his wife and daughter to continue what he began. The school motto – the Greek words for grace and knowledge – come at the end of Peter's second letter in the New Testament and I can think of no better way to end my final letter to all of you: "But grow in the grace and knowledge of our Lord and Saviour Jesus Christ. To him be the glory both now and for ever."

As my thirtieth and final year at Scarisbrick Hall School drew to a close, I received many letters and cards. Among the kind sentiments in one parent's letter were these words: 'For you personally, this is the end of an era in many ways. You must feel especially sad to be leaving such a wonderful school, when the school itself is, in effect, closing down.'

Some of the staff and pupils would carry on into the new era as part of Kingswood College. One girl, Jade Headley, was then completing Year 5, and, although her parents looked at possible alternative schools, she stayed on. She could have had no inkling that, ten years later, members of her family would be the ones to give Scarisbrick Hall School a rebirth.

The Bombshell

A birds-eye view of Scarisbrick Hall School

Jeff Shaw as Captain Von Trapp in The Sound of Music, 1997

CHAPTER 9
Renaissance

It is not within the present writer's remit to write in any detail about the twelve-year life of Kingswood College at Scarisbrick Hall. It is clear that the promised expenditure on building infrastructure was not delivered.

I know that a high proportion of my colleagues had moved on within three years. One who kept in touch was Mike Halewood, who gave many years' service as laboratory technician, as cricket team manager and as a guide and mentor to many young Christians in the school. He stayed as long as he could until he found that the circumstances of his employment changed to the point where he felt he could not continue. He found employment at St Mary's College in Crosby.

Some, however, did stay in the new set-up right through to the time when the Headley family took over. Jenny Whitfield, who had been Head of the Nursery department since 1992, continued under the new regime; as also did Heidi Sutcliffe, who at the time of writing had finally retired from teaching after forty years in the younger end of First School.

Other teachers looked to Tower College and Rachel Oxley for possible teaching vacancies. Two had transferred prior to the merger and one went as the merger happened. In the years that followed another six were able to move across; the fact that they went two by two prompted Rachel Oxley to compare Tower College to Noah's Ark as a place of refuge from the swirling waters of Kingswood College!

Nord Anglia had said, on taking over the running of the school, that up to a million pounds would be spent on necessary repairs to the fabric of the Hall. It became the practice, however, for rooms to be shut off rather than repaired. Most of the rooms in the main Hall were out of use by the time the Headley family took possession. Nord Anglia retained ownership of the school for six years, but in 2001 they shut down the Sixth Form and then, in 2004, they sold all their UK schools, including Kingswood College. The new owners were Global Education Management Services (GEMS). Jade Headley left that year at the age of sixteen, but her cousins were now pupils at the school.

In 2005 it was time for another inspection by a team from the Independent Schools Inspectorate (ISI). ISI is the body set up by the Independent Schools Council (ISC) to inspect schools that are members of the seven associations that make up the ISC. More than 1200 schools, represented by their Heads, Bursars or Governors, make up the ISC. ISI is a government approved inspectorate and the quality of its services is monitored by Ofsted on behalf of the Department for Education.

The ISI report on Kingswood College at Scarisbrick Hall in 2005 stated that the school had 407 pupils, of whom 203 were in the Senior School and a total of 99 had some form of special educational needs. Pupils were commended for their excellent behaviour; their learning and attitudes were also very good. Teaching, overall standards, curriculum and personal development were all good. Other comments, however, were less complimentary. Most departments, apart from ICT, were 'not well equipped' and resources were 'just adequate.' Teachers' morale had been lowered by speculation about the future and communication within the school was not good. The more able pupils were not being stretched, provision for health and safety was 'unsatisfactory' and progress since the last inspection was 'barely satisfactory.' The inspectors did take note of the fact that the lack of investment by previous owners adversely affected the state of the building. Whatever information they had about the history and the merger, they also felt it was necessary to make the judgement that 'the ethos of the two schools was totally different.'

Jade Headley's mother, Lynda, and aunt, Sue, had joined the Parents and Friends Association attached to Kingswood College. Initially two groups had separately committed themselves to raising funds for the school, but when they came together in one PFA, they elected Lynda as Chair and Sue as Secretary. Both women had business interests, Lynda with her partner Barry Cackett and Sue with her husband Greg Aylmer. Sue and Greg had three children, Ross, Zak and Chloe, who all attended Kingswood College. Lynda and Barry are the parents of Jade and Aaron.

Events suddenly seemed to lurch out of control. First of all, in November 2006, GEMS sold the Hall to property developers based in London. Then, in January 2007, GEMS announced that the school would close in July that year. It is important to hold on to the fact that ownership of the Hall did not include ownership of the school business. Indeed, the property developers had no idea that a school was operating within Scarisbrick Hall; they had never visited the estate or taken the trouble to discover what it was used for. It seems they may have hired a helicopter, flown over the site, liked the look of a Grade I listed building and, on the word of an intermediary, decided they could make it into a number of lucrative apartments.

At this point the PFA realised that action was needed if the education of up to 400 children was to be salvaged from the mess. A group of parents came together to form a charity – Kingswood College Trust – to manage the school, even if they might have to find alternative premises to do so, as the Hall had been sold. Although Jade Headley had left by now, she joined with her cousins Ross, Zak and Chloe to implore their respective parents and the wider family not to let the school die. Lynda and Greg – Sue's husband Greg Aylmer – joined the other parents who formed the Trust.

Enter Mike Headley

Mike Headley and his wife Linda (not to be confused with their daughter Lynda!) had thus far not been directly involved, although they were obviously concerned, and they heard the pleas of their grandchildren not to let the school just disappear. They had built up a very successful business providing care for vulnerable elderly people, but their focus was switching now to the needs of people at the opposite end of the age spectrum, also vulnerable but in a very different way. Lynda and Greg kept them up to date about the efforts of the Kingswood College Trust to save the school, but they recognised that the school without the Hall would be a very different creature.

By selling off their business, Mike and Linda had the wherewithal to join Lynda and Barry, and Sue and Greg, in making a serious attempt to buy back Scarisbrick Hall from the London-based developers and then not just to rescue the school, but to restore it to what it had once been and then perhaps to develop it into something even better. They even considered the possibility – if it proved impossible to buy back the Hall – of relocating the school in another venue. They did scout around for potential premises.

The developers were very difficult to pin down as to who actually owned the Hall, as there always seemed to be another company that was an offshoot from the company the Headleys thought they were dealing with. It took the Headley family two and a half years to convince the developers to sell Scarisbrick Hall. Everything smacked of the big boys in the big city failing to believe that a little guy from out in the provinces should be taken seriously. They had never met Mike Headley, but when they did, they found that his small physical stature concealed a huge amount of determination, perseverance and fighting spirit. He just would not go away.

On the cliff edge
Matters came to a head in a meeting in London to which Mike Headley was accompanied by daughter Lynda. To the developers, Scarisbrick Hall represented an investment opportunity. To hundreds of families in the Lancashire area it was the fulcrum of their educational world. When the Headleys produced a photograph of all the pupils, they felt as if they were standing on a cliff edge. Would the hard-headed business people maintain their insistence on prospective financial gain, or would they show a heart of compassion towards those children and their families? Finally, the developers gave in to the Headleys' pressure; they agreed to sell their business, of which Scarisbrick Hall was the main asset, to the Headley family.

The plan had always been for the school and the Hall to be under the same ownership, with a Board of Directors consisting of Mike as chair, with Linda, Sue, Greg, Lynda and Barry alongside. They were under no illusions about the size of the task confronting them in repairing and restoring the Hall. The task of rescuing and reviving the school was no less challenging. Their vision extended well beyond that, however, guided as they were by their united belief that 'the heart of Scarisbrick Hall belongs as a school, and the heart of the school belongs at Scarisbrick Hall.'

The Headleys were business people, not educationalists, so they sought help from people who could advise them as to the state of things in the school. Members of the Trust, who would visit the school every three months, had the impression that numbers and standards were being maintained. Mike Headley asked three of his friends who were head teachers to have a good look at the school and to ask some searching questions. What they found was quite alarming.

Crisis time
Numbers of pupils had fallen to 120, aged from three to sixteen. Classrooms needed decorating; garden areas of the grounds were turning into jungle; facilities for teaching and learning were dated and of poor quality; the teaching staff were demoralised. The Trust had no funds to undertake any kind of refurbishment. Neither the Oxley family nor Nord Anglia nor GEMS nor the Kingswood College Trust had been able to commit to the level of funding that was needed to put the Hall into sound condition and upgrade the whole infrastructure of the school. It is to the credit of Eric Borowski and some dedicated teachers that the school managed to keep going at all.

Several members of staff, understandably concerned about their future prospects, had consulted union representatives to try and safeguard their jobs. The unions, for their part, did not appear to believe that the Headleys would keep the school going once they had purchased the Hall. Conveyancing lawyers rarely seem to break speed records and the process of buying the school business from the Trust took longer than either side really wanted. The point came where the teaching unions set a deadline for completion, after which all members of staff would be issued with redundancy letters. Mike and Lynda Headley tried desperately to reassure everybody concerned that the sale would be completed in time, but on the day of the deadline, members of staff received their redundancy letters. By the end of the day the purchase was indeed completed and the letters were rescinded on the following day.

The first thing that Mr Headley did was to reinstate the name *Scarisbrick Hall School*; 'Kingswood College at Scarisbrick Hall' had lasted for twelve years, but the Headleys were determined to restore as much as they could of the school that Jade had experienced until 1998. Her uncle, Greg Aylmer, went to social media to put the word out to former pupils that the project was underway. He wrote about the family involvement, the acquisition of the Hall and the school and then went on: 'We have already made a number of improvements: the school has been renamed Scarisbrick Hall School and we have created a Scarisbrick Hall School page on Facebook. I would like you all to become a fan. We will be keeping the page updated as the restoration and refurbishments take place and hopefully one day it would be nice to see you all at the Hall.' One former pupil probably expressed the feelings of many when she commented: 'Fantastic – what a great project! When I visited a few years back I was heartbroken to see the sad state parts of it were in!'

Many people seeing the Hall and the grounds would have wanted to see money spent on it; the Headley family now had the job of sorting out their priorities and directing funds into the most essential parts of the project. Some unexpected outstanding debts from previous ownership also had to be settled.

One School & Two Families

On behalf of the family, Lynda Headley addressed parents and staff with these words:

> *Following the announcement by my family that we were to acquire Scarisbrick Hall and the school, we have since spent many weeks discussing the strategic plans for the development of our school and its home in Scarisbrick Hall, in particular the urgent works required to stop leaky roofs, improve the general appearance of the Hall and grounds whilst developing a plan for a full restoration of Scarisbrick Hall.*
>
> *When formulating these plans and agreeing the actions required to bring new life and energy into the tired and dilapidated areas of the Hall, we have also considered in what ways we can bring new life and energy into the educational experience that maximises the potential development of every child here.*
>
> *Therefore the commitment to our children is to do the very best we can today and to make each day new and exciting, full of potential and wonder at what we are all achieving as we rebuild this school with the latest in teaching and learning resources in a safe and secure environment within these beautiful grounds.*
>
> *Our priority is therefore for the children that are here now.*
>
> *Whilst I could stand here and present grand plans and slide shows regarding the future restoration of the Hall and the building of new facilities for the school, this is not the purpose of the day. Today we*

celebrate the achievements of our children and the dedication and skill of the staff in encouraging and securing their development throughout this last year.

Pugin inspired a vision and the Hall became manifest by the blood and sweat of others who shared in that vision.

The Headley family are not building this school. We have no interest in status or title. You all are the builders and each stone laid should be a part of a unifying vision of the greatness this school can be. We will therefore support each other and encourage the skill of the individuals that make up our school family.

Our school building has a tower that is seen for miles around standing out as a statement of its grandeur.

Our school body has a spire that reaches much higher than the eye can see. And as a statement of our purpose, this is a different kind of spire – one that is only limited by our imagination and commitment to the actions to build it.

We as parents, grandparents, management and staff ASPIRE – meaning to seek to attain a particular goal, to soar to a great height – so as to INSPIRE our children so that they can reach and be all that they want to be.'

Rotten rafters

A structural engineer soon spotted that the roof of the Great Hall was in danger of falling in. Water had clearly been coming in for years, because an oak beam, stretching the length of the

Great Hall and twelve inches thick, had largely disintegrated. This beam supported the rafters, and the lower ends of the rafters were also rotten. If the beam and the rafters were not replaced, the school would have to close down. The process of repair required the insertion of a metal beam to take the weight of the roof while the source of the leaks was located and the drying out could take place.

In addition to the expenditure required to make the Hall fit for purpose and the school operationally viable, the new owners also had to reckon with the very real human costs involved in the project. Some of the staff had been through rough times and the threat of closure had had its effects on morale. Pupils themselves would hardly have been aware of the stresses that their Head and other staff would have been under, but parents – especially those who had been members of the Trust – needed reassurance that the Headley family would fulfil their promises. The immediate outlay of about a million pounds on school resources went some way towards giving them that reassurance.

Eric Borowski was approaching retirement, but he agreed to continue as Director of Education while a new Head was appointed to start in September 2010. This person, who cannot be named for legal reasons, had little time to review all areas of school life, because at the end of March 2011, just six months after being appointed, along came a team of ISI inspectors.

The school now had 304 pupils of whom 188 were aged between birth and 11, with just 116 from 11 to 16. The 188 included EYFS nursery and pre-school children, some of whom attended for part-time childcare, so in reality the total of school age children was well below the 304 figure. The inspectors noted that the 70 children with special educational needs 'achieve exceptionally well.' Elsewhere, the ability range was wide, and the one-hour lessons were proving too long for some in the Junior and Senior schools. In response to the previous report, better teaching now stretched the more able pupils and 'huge investment in good quality resources' had led to greater confidence among parents and improved morale amongst the staff. Assessment no longer stood in isolation but related clearly to future planning. Extra-curricular activities in the daily timetable included canoeing, cookery, photography, sailing and self-defence. The school had an open door policy, with an invitation to parents to meet the Directors on Tuesday mornings over coffee.

The inspectors took note that the Directors had shown a 'robust response to the recommendations of the previous inspection to address urgently the many problems associated with the site and the buildings. The challenges of maintaining the Grade 1 listed building are considerable, but the directors are not daunted by the task and have a comprehensive business plan for the future of the site.'

Under the heading of governance and management, the inspection team recognised that the Directors were concerned about legal responsibilities, safeguarding, welfare, health and safety. 'An ambitious development plan has been drawn up by the directors in discussion with the Head, but as yet teachers have not contributed to it.' Also, specific responsibilities of management, including those of the directors, were not yet fully clear.

Closure?
When an ISI inspection is complete, the Reporting Inspector sends a report to the association of which the school is a member; in this case, it was the Independent Schools

Association. Inspections have in recent years given greater weighting than before to governance and management, particularly in regard to compliance with the increasingly complex web of regulations. On this occasion, the inspectors identified too many gaps in the necessary paperwork, too many boxes yet to be ticked. This occurred partly because the Head – who had no experience of leading a school under inspection – had unfortunately not given the inspection team a copy of the policies and procedures that the Headleys had put together. The overall judgement of governance and management by the inspectors declared it to be unsatisfactory. When that judgement landed on the desk of the Chief Executive Officer of the ISA, it brought a swift reaction: 'You have seven days to sort things out or I close the school down.'

This was a real body blow. If there is one thing for which Mike Headley and his daughters were sticklers, it is the whole area of policies, regulations and compliances. To succeed in the businesses they have developed, that has always been a high priority. To be told now that Scarisbrick Hall School was in breach of so many regulations really hurt them. All their plans and ambitions seemed to be tumbling around them. They felt that they had to be seen to be making swift amends for the unsatisfactory inspection report and acknowledged that they had perhaps placed a burden of expectation on their appointed Head which that person had not been able to meet in full. A change of leadership was necessary.

A news story that the school was looking for a new Head caught the attention of Jeff Shaw, whose links with Scarisbrick Hall School were substantial. He and his sister Jacky had both been pupils there and their mother had taught in both Scarisbrick and Tower College Junior departments. With a degree from the Royal Northern College of Music, a PGCE and

Renaissance

an MA in Educational Leadership, Jeff had held leadership roles in two schools in Cheshire before joining the staff of Edge Hill University, Ormskirk, where he became a Senior Lecturer and Assistant Head of Secondary Education. He had fond memories of his years at Scarisbrick Hall, and, having completed his schooling before the merger with Kingswood, he had no scars from the disruption of the transitional period. On reading of the departure of the Head, and being ready for a new challenge, he sent in his curriculum vitae to the Directors of Scarisbrick Hall School. They, in their turn, recognised that here was not only a very capable leader, but also someone with a wider and deeper understanding of education, something that the Headley family had been looking for.

The school already had a partnership arrangement with Edge Hill University. For many years, since the time when it was Edge Hill Teacher Training College, student teachers had been able to do teaching practice at Scarisbrick Hall.

Heads it is
In their planning for the future, the Directors wanted to divide leadership responsibility so that they would have a Head of the younger age range and a Head of the older segment. In the former role they appointed Tony McCoy, who had previously taught in the Junior School of Kingswood College before leaving to work in the state sector. The school would be divided into four parts: First School and Middle School, overseen by Tony McCoy; and College and Sixth Form, with Jeff Shaw in charge. Although in 2011 the school did not have a Sixth Form, it was very much part of the plan to reintroduce it as soon as possible.

The first priority for the Headley family was to clarify the values of the re-formed Scarisbrick Hall School. They agreed with Mr Shaw's statement, quoting Socrates, that 'Education is the kindling of the flame, not the filling of the vessel.' They approved of the Kingswood focus on the individual child rather than a broad-based, collective approach to teaching. They also wanted to keep fees within the range of middle income families, as it had always been among Charles and Muriel Oxlcy's primary objectives.

During July 2011, an advertisement for the Headships of Scarisbrick Hall School appeared in the *Times Educational Supplement.* Mr Shaw sent in a formal application at the end of the month; he was interviewed, and at the end of August he received the letter offering him the post of Head of the College and Senior School. He still had projects to complete at Edge Hill and handed in his notice there, enabling him to take up his new post after the October half-term holiday.

Most people would assume that in a school it is the pupils who learn and the teachers who teach. Jeff Shaw saw things rather differently. In a previous school he had led the redesign of the performance management system to integrate the notion of 'teacher learning.' All staff were expected to develop strategies to improve identified areas of weakness and also deliver workshops to other colleagues where success was identified. These strategies were closely monitored by line managers. Some teachers, who preferred their well-established teaching methods, did not like the new strategy, but as it began to produce positive results it gained acceptance.

In his previous roles Mr Shaw had been involved in pioneering work across the country and internationally with the Department for Education to improve school-based learning for both pupils and teachers. In the days before 'austerity' became the political byword, funding for research enabled him to travel abroad and to work with influential people in the UK as well. He grew in his own understanding of how to develop and motivate teachers.

He worked hard to help the Directors see that a school's values are absolutely fundamental to its success. Buildings, facilities, special events, the look of the place – all these were important, but what had always been the heartbeat of Scarisbrick Hall School was its values. What Jeff Shaw passionately believed in were high quality teaching and learning, high expectations of behaviour, and traditional family values. He initiated a drive for greater academic achievement from the start.

What he looked to establish at Scarisbrick Hall was a 'centralised benchmark of expectations for every lesson' and 'to develop what is expected for an "outstanding Scarisbrick Hall lesson". From the start of the lesson through to teaching strategies or themes right through to the way that students depart the room, the leadership team should be able to walk into any lesson and look for key expectations and values.' A teacher would still be able to show initiative and creativity, but by setting a benchmark the leadership would be able to take aspects of good practice from one subject area and apply it in others also.

Continuity and stability assumed great importance as the new regime found its feet in the school. Eric Borowski had seen the school through turbulent times, but the directors felt that they could move ahead without his involvement. He deserves much credit for not giving up when the Kingswood College project seemed to be collapsing irreparably.

A few teachers also provided continuity right through from the days of Kingswood School in Birkdale to the Headley regime of Scarisbrick Hall School: Jane Whitehouse, for example, in the Junior School, and Ina Taylor, who was Deputy Head of Kingswood College and was happy to continue as a Head of Year when the Scarisbrick renaissance took place. Staff and parents turned up in numbers to help the Headleys clean and decorate the place when the new regime began to operate.

CHAPTER 10
High Hopes

Inspectors return

Two groups of people needed to be convinced that the new regime could succeed. To commit a child into an independent school requires a long-term financial investment, and prospective parents look for reassurance that they will not be wasting their money. The other interested party is the inspectorate. Would a team from the Independent Schools Inspectorate be able to give their stamp of approval to the renewal of Scarisbrick Hall School? The answer came early in 2014, almost fifty years after the original school opened.

One thing to look for in an inspection report is how many items appear under a heading such as 'Action Points' or 'Recommendations for improvement.' The 2011 report, for example, had quite a long list of things that had not been up to scratch but were then being addressed, with five recommendations added. The 2014 report stated that those recommendations had been implemented in full, and the inspectors were clearly scratching around for anything they could include as items in need of attention.

ISI reports have until recently used four one-word categories of judgement: Excellent, Good, Sound and Unsatisfactory. Additionally, judgements for Early Years Foundation Stage (EYFS) – for children under three years old – are Outstanding, Good, Requires improvement and Inadequate. In the report on the inspection of Scarisbrick Hall

School in January 2014 the three paragraphs under the heading 'Main Findings' use the word 'Excellent' on twelve occasions. Aspects including achievement, curriculum, extra-curricular activities, teaching, personal development, pastoral care, relationships with other pupils and with staff, proprietors' support and oversight, results of pupils with special educational needs – all are rated excellent; 'provision and outcomes' in EYFS are rated outstanding. Superlatives abound throughout the more detailed findings in the report.

Having taken part in more than twenty ISI inspections as a team inspector, I cannot recall schools where responses to the parents' questionnaire were absolutely unanimous that they would recommend their school to other parents. Yet that is what Scarisbrick parents said. One might expect one or two parents with a bit of a grudge to take the opportunity to have a little niggle about something they do not like. That was not the case here, though. They were overwhelmingly positive about the care and the education that their offspring received.

With an inspection report such as the one given to Scarisbrick Hall School in 2014, it is difficult to argue with the proposition that the reborn school had already achieved notable success and had a strong basis from which to launch further forward in the future. Evidence suggests that there is no resting on laurels or easing back on the oars. To stand still is usually the herald of deterioration, and the Directors and Head had no intention of allowing that to happen. They were themselves raising the bar and widening the vision, challenging other establishments with what had already been accomplished and what was yet to appear, further down the line. In 2014 the Independent Schools Association bestowed a significant honour on the school when it was given the Senior School Award for Excellence and Innovation in Provision.

High Hopes

In 2015 the ISA also presented the school with its National Award for Excellence in sports provision. Internally, specialist PE teachers cover the full age range from pre-school to the Sixth Form. Additionally, the school has brought in specialist coaches in a range of sports, including, for example, a sports conditioning coach who educates on the physical, mental and nutritional requirements of high level sport. Pupils are not confined to their own sports field and gymnasium, as arrangements are made with the Burscough Sports Centre, the Ormskirk Park Pool and Edge Hill University's superb sports facilities for the benefit of the pupils. Also, a range of sports is available in the afternoon slot in the timetable for E3 – Extend, Enrich, Excite. The Beautiful Beginnings Day Nursery includes games and sport alongside art, music, role play, cooking, dance and the woodland learning environment.

The Duke of Edinburgh Award Scheme ties in well with the school's holistic approach to education, and the school has become an Independent Operating Authority for the Scheme. Local authorities have traditionally fulfilled this role, but in uncertain times, when budgets have had to be cut, there is no guarantee that Lancashire or Sefton will be able to continue their involvement.

Having contributed significantly to the turnaround in the school's fortunes, Tony McCoy left his position as Head of First and Middle Schools to become the Head of his own school. Jeff Shaw would now continue as overall Head of Scarisbrick Hall, with the support of a First School management team.

For Mr Shaw to be able to run the school effectively, he needed strong support from the Directors, which he has always had. The Directors are a family and a team, spanning generations and building a legacy for future generations as well. Mike and Linda Headley, the senior members of the family by age, were keen to have it recognised that theirs was just one part of the growing enterprise that is Scarisbrick Hall School. Alongside them are two daughters and one son, plus partners, and the third generation also.

Sue dealt with policies, procedures and day-to-day business governance, and since the death of Mike Headley, she has taken on the responsibility of Chair of Directors. Her husband, Greg, is the financial director, dealing with investment and working closely with English Heritage on the building refurbishment and future planning. They have three children: Ross, studying PE and Management and already running his own company; Zak, having left school and now learning the ropes on the extensive maintenance side of the school and its buildings and grounds; and Chloe, who was also a pupil at the school.

Sue's sister is Lynda, who oversees recruitment. Lynda's husband, Barry, has his own business interests that are not directly linked to the school, although he is a strong supporter of the work. Their son, Aaron, is an entrepreneur and their daughter Jade is actively involved in the school's holiday club and sports development, particularly in netball.

Mike and Linda's son, Lee, has an important role in maintenance and repairs around the school buildings and grounds.

With three generations of the family already 'hands on', the intention is that as the years progress, so something of a dynasty will be established. The vision is for each generation to grow up through the school in their younger years, then take on necessary roles to maintain continuity and standards of excellence.

Standards upheld
As we have seen, the Independent Schools Inspectorate (ISI) conducts its own inspections on a regular basis. However, if a

school undergoes a 'material change', then the Department for Education steps in to ensure that the Government's standards are being maintained. In 2015, therefore, when Scarisbrick Hall School indicated its intention of reintroducing a Sixth Form, DfE inspectors arrived to check whether the school had the necessary facilities and staffing arrangements to accommodate Sixth Form students. They gave their approval.

Similarly, as the numbers of pupils had risen from 130 to 620 over a period of six years, the DfE had to be satisfied that this was no imposition of a regime in which, say, one teacher was attempting to teach sixty children in a class in Dickensian cramped conditions. A visit from DfE inspectors in 2017 confirmed that the school catered well for appropriate class sizes in well-appointed classrooms and conditions.

Examination results have shown an upward trend in recent years. The focus these days is on the percentage of pupils achieving top grades. Between 2014 and 2017, the percentage of subject passes with grades A*, A or B by Scarisbrick pupils at GCSE rose from 61% to 74%; those at A*/A rose from 35% to 47%. In 2017 every candidate achieved at least five A*–C passes. The average number of subject passes per candidate was 8.9.

At GCE Advanced Level the first cohort of the reintroduced Sixth Form all entered for three subjects each and achieved a 100% pass rate.

Family values
The history of Scarisbrick Hall School, as we have seen, has depended very much on two families, the Oxleys and the Headleys, who between them have enthused hundreds of parents, pupils and teachers to join them in the adventure of building something special and probably unique.

One School & Two Families

In the illustrious history of a football club such as Manchester United, with its triumphs and its tragedies, it is understandable that observers make comparisons between the eras of, say, Sir Matt Busby and Sir Alex Ferguson. The aim was always success on the field and, especially in more recent times, success as a global brand. The list of trophies won is impressive, but it would perhaps be invidious to make too close a comparison between Busby and Ferguson as to how they achieved success. Both were men of vision, passion, determination, even ruthlessness at times, in their pursuit of glory. Yet each man had his own style, his own priorities and his own modus operandi.

Something similar could apply equally to Charles and Muriel Oxley and Mike and Linda Headley. For the Oxleys, it was a pioneering project from scratch; for the Headleys, a rescue and a renewal, with an ongoing vision and exciting development plans. What they shared is a desire to see children and young people growing up equipped with values and standards to have a wholesome influence on the world around them and to find the satisfaction of a well-rounded life.

So how does Scarisbrick Hall School Mark II compare with the original? Does it have the same values, the same standards, the same expectations? Has the Headley model replicated the Oxley prototype, or are they both unique – and therefore different?

Premises
To one who came up the main drive in 1964 and then returned in 2024, a first glance might suggest that little had changed. Radical alterations to a Grade 1 listed neo-Gothic nineteenth-century mansion simply cannot happen. The stream still flows into the lake and then runs away over a weir and out into the

High Hopes

wider Scarisbrick estate. The top of the tower still peeps above the surrounding trees to become a focal point for miles around the West Lancashire landscape.

A closer look, however, would reveal the changes. At the fork, opposite the entrance to the Girl Guides campsite, a car park has been established in the upper section of the woodland. It was laid out at the latter end of the Oxley era to give a safe meeting point for pupils whose parents were bringing them and taking them home by car. What once was a lawn outside the west wing of the Hall is another car park, for visitors. And where there used to be four hard tennis courts in the garden area is now the staff car park. All of this means that the turning circle in front of the main entrance to the Hall is now free of traffic and parked cars, thus maintaining the splendid aspect of the south-facing frontage.

The present administration clearly has a much greater reservoir of funding than any of its predecessors. They have put that money to outstandingly good use. There is little point trying to repair a hernia with a sticking-plaster, and the Headleys have spared no expense in, firstly, putting right the problems with the structure of the Hall and, secondly, refurbishing and bringing back into use parts of the building that had been unable to be used for years.

Their commitment has recently extended into significant new building developments such as the performing arts complex. For many years, the school gymnasium – built in the era of St Katherine's College – served as an occasional theatre, with a basic stage and a proscenium. In the later years of the Oxley era, temporary, free-standing staging could be added to allow for larger casts and more movement in the musicals that the school presented. A purpose-built auditorium became more than a pipe dream in 2019, when plans were drawn up and the project was set to go. Then COVID happened: plans had to be shelved, but certainly not abandoned.

The Oak Theatre performing arts facility, opened in 2023, includes a 400-seater auditorium, with retractable seating; rehearsal rooms, a recording studio and dance studio; and rooms for individual music lessons and practice. Former pupils of a certain age may be astonished to learn that what has served as a pump room, a pottery room and a girls' changing room in successive generations is now a restaurant central to this performing arts area. Sixth formers may sit in there with their books and/or laptop and engage in private study in a relaxed, undergraduate style atmosphere. The Oak Theatre facility will not only meet the school's needs as a venue for school assemblies and other occasions such as Sixth Form lectures, but it will also attract the wider community, as this beautiful complex will be available for local groups to use throughout the year.

One noticeable change in approach in the twenty-first century has been the return of teaching to the Hall building itself. First-floor rooms, some of which had originally been classrooms, later served as dormitories in the days of boarders. Classes were then moved out as numbers increased and were taught in the purpose-built single-storey blocks behind the Hall building. When pupil numbers hit 700, the Oxleys erected prefabricated buildings to house extra classes; the official line was that these were temporary but they remained useful for many years. As the boarding complement declined and then disappeared, rooms in the Hall were left empty. Briefly in the 1980s, some of them were occupied by Liverpool Bible College. Today, however, it is the policy of the school to use all available rooms in the main Hall building for teaching.

High Hopes

The Great Hall was for a few years used as a conference room, with a large screen available to make presentations. In addition to eminent university academics who have visited to give lectures to senior students, the school has had the distinction of hosting a Royal Society lecture. Such events are now housed in the Oak Theatre, and the Great Hall now has comfortable seating for mentoring, parents' evenings and individual conversations. A beautiful new carpet has been installed, incorporating design features of the Hall. To those who might question the need for a carpet, the answer is that it protects – not hides – the mosaic work underneath.

The Red and Blue Drawing Rooms came into use only on special occasions during the Oxley era; now, they are in regular use as classrooms, as also is what used to be the boarders' common room, now referred to as the Green Room. Lady Ann's bedroom on the first floor is now an office for the Directors. A very impressive development has been the transformation of some of the former Kindergarten rooms in the courtyard into state-of-the-art science laboratories. To install a new staircase there meant a lengthy battle with planners, but it definitely enhances that block, as does the signage in and around the laboratories. During the Headships of Mr Oxley and Mr Raynor, the Head's office was adjacent to Reception, but during the Kingswood era it moved behind the main corridor; now it has returned to its former location for Mr Shaw.

What used to be called the 'back corridor' by some and 'G corridor' by others had to be blocked off for years because of the dilapidated condition of the roof. Fresh vision – and a sizeable financial investment – has transformed first-floor bedrooms and a ground floor room immediately below them that once served in different decades as both chemistry lab and staffroom. The bedrooms must have been built in the time of St Katherine's College; their ceiling was actually a false one, which, when removed, not only revealed asbestos but also amazed the Headleys. Up above appeared another arched ceiling, similar in style to the one in the Great Hall, though not as big. Once the asbestos had been safely removed, the next problem was the inevitable bats, which caused a delay in the planned development. But the vision has now become reality: two libraries.

The senior library occupies the arch-ceilinged space where boarders' bedrooms once stood on the first floor; the junior library downstairs fills the former staffroom (previously chemistry lab) on the ground floor. The senior library has been named The Roberts Library, in memory of the much-respected English teacher, Mr Steve Roberts, who died suddenly in January 2015. Members of his family were present when the Library was officially opened in January 2017 by Lord Hastings of Scarisbrick.

More classrooms and an additional staircase have been created where the Careers and Deputy Head's room and uniform office used to be, in that part of the building that is now officially known as the North Range. The conservationists and guardians of heritage could not see the need for the new staircase; fortunately, the fire service could, and their view prevailed with the planning department.

Real innovation has taken place in other areas. As you stand facing the front of the Hall, with the lake behind you, the arched gateway into the courtyard stands to your right. Go through the archway, turn right and open a door in the wall on your right. Those who were pupils in the Oxley era would expect to see mowing machines and other groundsman's equipment stored inside. But now you will find a mystical, magical place where classes can come and have their creative instincts stimulated. It is called the Story-telling Tower. The only natural light comes from the opened door, so once that is closed the room might at first seem a little scary; but there are LED lights and seats and a variety of puppets and other 'props' that teachers can use to help pupils create a story. The room is circular, lined with bricks up to about thirty feet. Lighting effects can create a campfire feeling, which helps to give any class group a sense of togetherness. The Story-telling Tower is more than a pleasant place to be creative, as the work done in there is always followed up back in the classroom.

Another initiative for making the best use of the Hall grounds is the Outdoor Learning Environment. An area of woodland stretches from near the fork in the front drive, all the way down behind the former science block to the visitors' car park alongside the west wing of the Hall. The patch immediately behind the old science block has been cleared of undergrowth to create an area where all kinds of activities take place. All classes up to the age of 11 spend time there, but not just for the enrichment value; classes up to Year 4 have timetabled lessons in the Forest School, with teaching assistants doing valuable work, similar to laboratory technicians in the science department, to prepare the detailed programme for the pupils and teachers to use.

The single-storey classroom and science blocks erected during the 1970s have suffered regularly from having flat roofs, with leaks almost inevitable from time to time. They have continued to serve well as classrooms for younger age groups, but plans are in hand for them to be gradually replaced in the coming years with new two-storey buildings.

Sanctions

Earlier generations of Scarisbrick pupils and their parents would notice a different approach to 'crime and punishment' under the present regime.

In Charles Oxley's *Pupils' Guides*, he spelled out the kind of behaviour that would not be tolerated, but did not specify what would happen to a transgressor. Because of his battles with groups and individuals who opposed corporal punishment, he gained a reputation as a frequent user of the cane. This was wrong on two counts: firstly, the means of applying corporal punishment was never a stick or cane, but more likely a slipper; secondly, after the early years when he felt the need to come down hard on miscreants in order to establish standards, use of the slipper became much more rare. Scarisbrick Hall School was still officially able to use corporal punishment even after it had been banned in state schools, but the need for it was so rare that it had pretty well disappeared by the time of the 1998 merger. Kingswood School and Kingswood College at Scarisbrick Hall never used corporal punishment.

'It has long been established that rewards are far more effective than punishment in motivating pupils.' This statement appears in the eighteen-page 'Behaviour Policy' of the twenty-first century version of Scarisbrick Hall School. The policy declares that staff will use physical intervention as an act of care and control and never punishment. It also emphasises the value of praise, positive reinforcement, rewards and celebration. Sanctions are available to deal with misbehaviour if and when it occurs.

High Hopes

Mike Headley

Linda Headley School Director

Lynda Headley School Director

Sue Aylmer School Director

Greg Aylmer School Director

One School & Two Families

One Headmaster greets another

High Hopes

Former Junior School playground with pottery room (left) and courtyard (back right) before the Performing Arts development

Opening of the library by Lord Michael Hastings

One School & Two Families

The new school library

The restoration of the tower

CHAPTER 11
PANDEMIC PROBLEMS

Coronavirus

No history of the school would be complete without recording the impact of COVID 19 on Scarisbrick Hall School.

The coronavirus that spread across the world from Wuhan in China late in 2019 had a devastating effect on millions of lives. In addition to the dreadful numbers of fatalities, every sphere of human activity seems to have been affected by the pandemic. Schools were suddenly faced with a complicated series of dilemmas for which nobody could be completely trained or prepared. Scarisbrick Hall was no exception.

Imagine being a naval captain in charge of a large ship, with hundreds of passengers on board, with only one working engine, in the middle of a hurricane and running very close to hidden rocks that could sink the ship. Such might be the image to compare to the situation of Mr Shaw, the Headmaster.

The government decreed that schools must close, with the exception that the children of key workers should continue to attend and be educated. Where possible, children staying at home should have online teaching. Not unexpectedly, the children in independent schools proved to be better equipped in terms of technology than their state school counterparts, many of whom, particularly in deprived areas, had zero access initially to any kind of computer.

One School & Two Families

One major blessing in Mr Shaw's situation was that, shortly before the pandemic struck, the school had invested in a new piece of software that enabled him to see at a glance the class, the attendance, the test results, the subjects being taken, for every child in the school. The data proved invaluable in plotting a course of action, which the school had in place within twenty-four hours. Teachers would, as far as possible, be on the premises, whilst observing the rules about masks and social distancing. If they had to be at home supervising their own offspring, they were expected to deliver online teaching.

The school provided parents with a forty-page booklet to help them understand the school's actions and expectations. The Blue Drawing Room became a call centre, manned by staff advising anxious parents about all aspects of legal requirements and lockdown procedures.

Financial considerations were huge, both for the school and for many parents. Could the school reasonably expect parents to pay full fees in the lockdown, when the parents themselves were saddled with the responsibility of childcare? Many independent schools parents have their own businesses, mainly small to medium-sized: if those businesses were unable to operate, with employees furloughed and premises and machinery closed down, how could such parents afford to pay school fees?

The school had to be quite hard-nosed by saying in effect: If we don't have fees income, the school can no longer function and will have to close down. At the same time, Mr Shaw was always willing to talk to individual parents about their financial difficulties and to arrange a period of deferment of fees, although parents had to realise that eventually the fees would have to be paid. There were even instances of families struggling so desperately that the school sent out supplies of food and other essentials.

The sad reality of the pandemic was that some pupils had to be withdrawn from the school, as even the possibility of deferred fees payment could not mitigate the desperate financial straits that some parents experienced. It is ironic, but a fact, that new admissions outnumbered withdrawals, as parents recognised how well independent schools generally, and Scarisbrick Hall School in particular, responded to the huge challenges of COVID 19.

Staff were understandably fearful for their own future – not just teachers, because the school employed more than 200 people in a whole range of capacities. For example, Mr Shaw had to tell a meeting of minibus drivers that he could not guarantee their continuing employment.

Government decisions – whether legal requirements or 'just guidance' – often impacted schools with almost zero time for preparation. A press conference on Friday at 5.00 p.m. would be used to announce measures that had to be implemented first thing on Monday morning. When vaccines became available, the government wanted schools to push parents and their children to be vaccinated, but morally and legally that was not something the Directors and Mr Shaw felt they could do. If the school had strongly recommended vaccination and something went wrong for just one pupil, then the school would have been legally liable. One example of help that was kindly offered to the school came from a former Scarisbrick pupil, Dr Sujoy Biswas, who made his GP practice available for parents to contact about matters that school staff were not qualified to address.

In the second lockdown, Scarisbrick Hall staff provided a fully co-ordinated school day, as close to a normal day as possible, including registration by technology. If a child did not register online, there would very quickly be an enquiry from the school as to the child's whereabouts. For those pupils who attended school in person, the government's proposed strategy of pupil 'bubbles' proved to be impractical, particularly when siblings were in different bubbles but were obviously going to be together at home. The school did try, marking out separated play areas on the playing field.

When eventually life began to return to normal as the deadliness of the virus receded, it still took time for all members of the school community to readjust and regain a complete sense of wellbeing. Lengthy periods of life away from structures and routines become a new norm, and it takes great patience and careful attention to re-establish good practice and mental wellbeing. And for some, coping with a bereavement adds hugely to the trauma of the whole experience.

Bringing the world together
Whilst the coronavirus was a challenging period for all, the Headley family found a way to prove – as they have done throughout their business careers and in their time at Scarisbrick Hall School - that in uncertainty there is opportunity. One day, when Mike Headley and Jeff Shaw were discussing the effect of COVID on children across the world, they decided they wanted to give children a voice globally on the issues surrounding coronavirus and other topics. Through their networks and with support from former pupil Lord Michael Hastings, they arranged discussions with the leaders of the World Health Organisation and UNICEF to discuss their proposal.

After a period of discussions and a Zoom call with the Director General of the World Health Organisation, Dr Tedros

Adhanom Ghebreyesus, the Global Classroom was born. That was how, from an independent school in the countryside of West Lancashire, a programme was set up to bring together children across the world via cyberspace. At the time of writing, the Global Classroom has hosted ten episodes over the past four years with amazing worldwide outreach and success. This has included episodes with NASA discussing the James Webb telescope and Mars Rover project, regular discussions with National Geographic, and features from world-famous celebrities and other notable speakers and organisations.

To highlight the range of the project, the Global Classroom received over 140 million hits on the content it produced during 2021.

Before his passing Mike Headley regularly discussed one of his favourite moments of the Global Classroom. They successfully had an iPad delivered to a school in Cambodia; and it was Scarisbrick Hall pupils who had provided funds to build that school in a village from which a student was now able to ask a world leader a question.

The Global Classroom could not have succeeded without the technical support of two members of the school staff, Gareth Norbury and Keith Garlick, whose input went well beyond their job specification. Some episodes registered more than two million views at once!

The Global Classroom has also provided ongoing opportunities for students at Scarisbrick Hall, such as the following:

- Singer/songwriter Heather Small attending the school after her Global Classroom episode to discuss song-writing and music with those passionate about the subject

- Gold medal-winning heptathlete Dame Denise Lewis hosting a private seminar with Scarisbrick Hall students on the challenges for sports men and women
- A private seminar from NASA discussing the world's first images returned from the James Webb Telescope.

CHAPTER 12
Looking Ahead

A Successful Business

Another comparison between the Oxley and Headley eras is the scale of the respective business ventures. Charles Oxley always said that a school must be viable as a business; otherwise, all its plans and aspirations will fail. Bear in mind that Charles and Muriel Oxley went to the absolute limit of what they could afford in securing a bank loan to buy the Hall for £24,500 in 1963. Although they both had an understanding of the commercial world from their family backgrounds and Muriel's ongoing photography work, they certainly did not have large sums to invest. Indeed, they had to be quite frugal initially, buying up second-hand school furniture and avoiding waste with a passion. Nevertheless, they did establish a flourishing school and a successful business that had strength and growth for many years. It was only in the final phase before the 1998 merger that fees income alone could not put necessary structural repair work into effect and at the same time keep the school running. In the period of merger, neither Nord Anglia nor GEMS were able to commit the necessary sums of money to maintain, let alone develop, the school.

Since 2010 the picture has changed. Business success on a very different scale has enabled the Headley family to commit large sums to the repair and restoration of the Hall and to the development of the school. One outstanding (literally) example of the financial commitment is the total restoration of the tower.

This has been finally completed, with very minimal support from English Heritage, at a cost of approximately two million pounds to the Headley family. Such expenditure on a renowned and unique feature does not directly benefit the education going on below, but it clearly maintains and enhances the environment in which the school is able to operate.

The Directors have also opened up investment opportunities to those who would also like to put money into children's future. A ten-year development plan shows the extent of the Headleys' aspirations in striving to make the school unrivalled in its provision and its standards.

A Scarisbrick Hall education in the 2020s uses the acronym RIVER (Resilience, Independence, Values, Exploration and Reflection). High academic standards are still very much part of the package, with results in public examinations establishing the school firmly among the very best, not only in the North-West of England but also nationally. A wide range of activities is available for youngsters to take up.

The school employs full-time coaches in rugby, football, netball, and strength-and-conditioning; that is on top of P.E. staff in the regular curriculum. It has long been accepted that pupils may be out of normal classroom lessons for individual tuition in a musical instrument; so why not apply the same principle to the individual development of sporting prowess? For the school to be named as Lancashire Rugby School of the Year in 2022-23 bears witness to the effectiveness of this additional sports provision. Not every child will become an elite athlete, but every child can raise their standards if the willingness and the expertise are there.

Expansion is happening across the board. Beautiful Beginnings offers childcare for babies and pre-school toddlers. The Sixth Form is already well established and increasing in numbers. In September 2024 the school had its largest ever Year 12 (Lower Sixth) intake. Boarding is very much on the agenda, with plans already in place to have purpose-built accommodation for boarding Sixth Formers in a style similar to university halls of residence. Scarisbrick Hall pupils are encouraged to see their role in the wider world. To that end, the school has added Gold to the Bronze and Silver of the Duke of Edinburgh Awards available to pupils. Sixth Form students have spent time in Thailand working to help people whose lives were severely affected by the tsunami in 2004. They will also be involved in a project in India. The school leaders feel it is important for their pupils to experience a world beyond their privileged existence.

A pioneer's passing
Everyone connected with Scarisbrick Hall School was saddened by the news in November 2021 that Mr Michael Headley had passed away, after a brave battle with cancer. His contribution to the rescue and reinvigoration of the school cannot be overstated. Yes, it is very much a family project, but, alongside his wife Linda, the head of that family was Mike Headley, who was the Chair of the Directors of the school from 2010 onwards.

When Mike realised that cancer was going to take him out of the picture, he called a family gathering to London, where he was being treated. 'Family' included Jeff Shaw, with his wife and daughters. Mike wanted to reaffirm his vision and values, and to reassure those present that his imminent passing represented not so much an ending as the opening of a new chapter in the development of the school.

Mike and Linda's daughter, Sue, took over the reins as Chair of Governors/Directors. That change required the Department for Education to carry out a detailed enquiry as to her suitability for that role. She has maintained her parents' focus on this being a family commitment across the generations.

Also present at the London gathering were Mike and Linda's grandchildren, as this is a multi-generational project. Since Mike's passing, Ross, Zak, Jade, and Aaron have all taken on greater responsibility in maintaining the business's continued success and development.

Such was Mike's passion for Scarisbrick Hall that Linda knew he would love to visit Scarisbrick Hall one more time. As he made one final loop around the roundabout at the front of school he was met with a round of applause from groups of current and former parents, pupils, staff, and the local community, a clear sign of the reinvigoration of life he had provided to this school and its wider community.

His funeral service also heavily featured Scarisbrick Hall, the eulogy being read by current headmaster Jeff Shaw and the closing prayer was read by the 2021-2022 Head Boy and Head Girl, Dominic Stevenson and Amelia McKeown.

The Headley family would not claim to have the strong evangelical Christian faith of Charles and Muriel Oxley, but they appointed a Christian headmaster in Jeff Shaw and they gladly include, for example, a Christmas carol service in the school calendar, and a Christian Fellowship is one of the cultural activities on offer. The school's literature includes references to wellbeing, which relates to such concepts as self-reflection, personal identity, diversity, 'British values' and understanding other cultures.

Houses and Alumni
The school originally had Houses named after respected Bible scholars whose support was appreciated by Mr and Mrs Oxley:

Looking Ahead

Allen, Bruce, Elwood, and Martin. Following the merger in 1998, it was decided to have Houses reflecting the background of the two schools: Poulton and Wyburn from Kingswood; Oxley and Raynor from Scarisbrick. As the Kingswood element has now receded in relevance, there has been another partial renaming of the Houses, each of which also has a botanical emblem, reflecting the beautiful environment in which the school is situated. Oxley [tulip] and Raynor [bluebell] have now been joined by Headley [daffodil] and Pugin [oak].

In my time as Headmaster, I occasionally had prospective parents asking if the school had any celebrities among its alumni. It was, and is, my belief that the unassuming input of hundreds of former pupils in all kinds of ways to the good of society across the world is far more important than just those who have achieved public acclaim. Nevertheless, we can point to some who have become well known in various spheres. Reference was made earlier to the Hastings brothers, particularly Michael [now Baron Hastings of Scarisbrick].

Daniel Hastings' sphere of expertise he himself described simply as 'space', when visiting Scarisbrick in July 2024 – his first time back in 52 years! He became Head of the Department of Aeronautics and Astronautics at MIT (Massachusetts Institute of Technology), one of the most prestigious universities in the world, in 2019. He has served as chief scientist of the US Air Force, also on the National Science Board and with NASA; and, among many honours, was awarded membership of the National Academy of Engineering in recognition of his contributions in spacecraft, space system architecture and leadership in aerospace research and education.

Louise Ekland (nee Crone) has become a frontline presenter on French television, covering events such as the Cannes Film

161

Festival and the Paris Olympic Games 2024. She also had a light-hearted book published, in French – *God Save My Queen* – at the time of Her Majesty's platinum jubilee, to help republican French people to understand why our Queen was so special to her. Louise returned to Scarisbrick Hall to deliver the keynote speech for the 2024 academic year Awards Day, focusing on the strong foundation Scarisbrick Hall had given her.

Nisha Katona (nee Biswas) was a successful barrister for twenty years before embarking on a remarkable business enterprise, bringing 'real' Indian street food to towns and cities across the UK. The Mowgli chain of restaurants embodies a strong charitable ethic, and Nisha herself has also become a popular television chef. She is the Chancellor of Liverpool John Moores University and is committed to the development of two girls' schools in India.

Tommy Fleetwood was a Kingswood pupil who came to Scarisbrick in the merger. He is a highly ranked professional golfer, three times a European Ryder Cup team member; he has twice represented Great Britain in the Olympic Games, winning the silver medal in Paris 2024. He has enjoyed considerable success on the DP World Tour. In the world of professional golf, it is quite an accolade to be known simply by one's first name, such as Seve or Tiger. Everyone knows who 'Tommy' is; everyone speaks highly of his character.

Trudi Abadi was awarded the BEM in 2017 and an OBE in 2024 for her work in the National Crime Agency.

Sarah Graham (nee Vandevelde) – whose mother Helen was a member of staff at Scarisbrick – received an MBE from King Charles in 2024 for her superb organising of over 50 families and 155 volunteers in the villages of Buckinghamshire to host and house Ukrainian refugees immediately after the Russian invasion.

We can be sure that many others have distinguished themselves in a variety of spheres over the past 60 years.

The staff list no longer includes the name of Heidi Sutcliffe, who retired in 2022, the last of the teachers from the Oxley era. The current longest-serving staff member is Wendy Willis, who has worked in the catering department for 27 years. Wendy is regularly mentioned by recent alumni as a caring and friendly face from their time at school.

The staff list includes, at the time of writing, five teachers and a librarian who were pupils at the school, three of them in the same class! It has been a source of great satisfaction to the writer of this book that one of my sons is on the teaching staff, and a grandson served for two years as a teaching assistant.

Inspection

In early November 2022, a team of ISI inspectors arrived at the school for a full-scale check on 'Focused Compliance and Educational Quality.' Their conclusion confirmed that the school met all regulatory standards and requirements, which is in itself quite an achievement. However, what followed those bald headline statements in the inspection report makes good reading. The words 'excellent' and 'outstanding' appeared with amazing regularity. From babies right through to Sixth Form, the educational provision and the standards of teaching and learning simply could not be faulted. It was therefore no surprise to read that 'almost all pupils attain grades significantly higher than expected for those of their ability.'

The inspectors noted that in the 2022 public examinations, 50% of A Level grades were either A or A*; and in GCSE two thirds of grades were at the very top: 7 – 9. They commended the RIVER philosophy, the E3 activities and the use of outdoor learning. They found pupils to be considerate, self-confident, motivated and co-operative. Directors, staff, pupils and parents had good reason to be proud of what the school represents. Pupil numbers already exceeded 800, with up to four classes in each year group.

As noted elsewhere, the Headleys' vision for the school is a family enterprise down the generations. They are business people, so they gratefully include the academic input from the Shaws in that family concept. Not just Jeff, as Headmaster, but his wife, Rachel, who is also on the teaching staff, and their daughters, Josie and Tessa. Jeff is highly regarded across the independent school sector. He has served as Chairman of the Independent Schools Association during the pandemic and again in 2023-24. The ISA now comprises 651 schools and is the largest of the associations of independent schools in the UK.

*

Charles and Muriel Oxley, succeeded by their daughter Rachel, set out in 1964 with vision and vigour to create a school with high academic standards, high standards of behaviour, and an understanding of the Christian faith. Hundreds of former pupils and their parents will have looked back to those thirty-four years – some nostalgically, some perhaps with regrets; all, one hopes, with a measure of gratitude.

Since the Headley family took on the challenge in 2010, their focus was not just on repairing an historic building, but also on creating an establishment that would build on former excellence for generations to come. They have already achieved a remarkable amount. At the time of writing, several possibilities were being pursued for the further development of the school's curriculum and facilities. The threat of punitive tax impositions by the newly elected Labour government in 2024 has required careful planning, but no limitation of creative thinking or energy to reach new levels of excellence and provision.

The Oxleys and the Headleys have faced and overcome many challenges; the vision and the vigour have not diminished from one family to the other. The tower of the Hall may be regarded as a symbol of aspiration, pointing above the trees to a future that may not be cloudless, but will surely be bright.

One School & Two Families

-The new Oak Theatre Complex incorporating the former Pottery Room

Most recent birds-eye view of the whole school

Looking Ahead

Four generations of the Headley family

The launch of Global Classroom with Jeff Shaw, seated, and Mike Headley, foreground right